2011

WORLD INVESTMENT AND POLITICAL RISK

World Investment Trends and Corporate Perspectives

Government Takings and Expropriations

The Political Risk Insurance Industry

TABLE OF CONTENTS

BOXES

TABLES

FIGURES

FOREWORD

The mission of the Multilateral Investment Guarantee Agency (MIGA) is to promote foreign direct investment (FDI) into developing countries to support economic growth, reduce poverty, and improve people's lives. As part of this mandate, the agency seeks to foster a better understanding of investors' perceptions of political risk as they relate to FDI, as well as the role of the political risk insurance (PRI) industry in mitigating these risks.

Today's economic turbulence and fragility in developed countries are again posing challenges for the global economy. Developing countries are feeling the impact through multiple channels, including through the flows of FDI and private capital. Having rebounded sharply in 2010, FDI flows to developing countries continued to increase in 2011, but are expected to moderate going forward.

This uncertain economic landscape aside, developing countries are expected to grow more than twice as fast as high-income economies over the next few years. This continued growth, together with stronger and more business-friendly environments, should enhance their appeal to multinational enterprises worldwide.

While the views of the companies surveyed for this report confirm this, they also highlight growing investor concern about the state of the global economy and possible financing constraints.

The report highlights once again the salience of political risk as an important concern for multinational enterprises that seek to invest in developing countries. This is also reflected in the increased issuance of new political risk insurance in 2010, a trend that seems to be continuing in 2011, helped by a growing awareness of insurance as a risk-mitigation tool. This year the report also pays special attention to the FDI picture in the Middle East and North Africa region in light of the Arab Spring, as well as the reaction of multinational enterprises to these developments.

This year's report puts a spotlight on expropriation, a political risk with a long and recurring history, and examines motivations of host-country governments in deciding whether to expropriate. The report also highlights the role of political or economic shocks in triggering expropriations. It finds that investor disputes are more likely to be resolved by democratically elected governments rather than non-democratic regimes. This suggests that the propensity to expropriate is significantly higher in countries with non-democratic regimes, a finding that should be of interest to investors who are more concerned about political stability than about regime type and political institutions.

In today's turbulent world, we hope that this report sheds light on different dimensions of political risk and the role of investment insurance in fostering an environment conducive to attracting FDI and promoting development.

Izumi Kobayashi
Executive Vice President

ACKNOWLEDGMENTS

This report was prepared by a team led by Daniel Villar and comprising Nathan Jensen (Associate Professor, Department of Political Science, Washington University in St. Louis), Persephone Economou, and Moritz Zander. Inputs were received from Manabu Nose. Mallory Saleson, Rebecca Post, and Cara Santos Pianesi edited the report. Suzanne Pelland was in charge of graphic design. Saodat Ibragimova, Melissa Johnson, and Vladislav Ostroumov provided administrative support.

The report benefitted from comments by MIGA's senior management team comprising Izumi Kobayashi, Michel Wormser, Edith P. Quintrell, Marcus Williams, Ravi Vish, Ana-Mita Betancourt, Kevin Lu, and Lakshmi Shyam-Sunder. Within MIGA, comments were also received from Marc Roex, Jonathan Halpern, Paul Barbour, Connor Healy, Franciscus Linden, Mario Marchesini, Stephan Dreyhaupt, Mikael Sundberg, and Aradhana Kumar-Capoor.

The World Bank's Development Prospects Group, under the guidance of Andrew Burns, provided the macroeconomic data presented in the report. The investor survey was conducted on behalf of MIGA by the Economist Intelligence Unit. The analysis of the political risk insurance market benefited from the gracious participation of political risk brokers in a roundtable discussion in London organized by Exporta Publishing and Events Ltd. Arthur J. Gallagher & Co. provided data on the private insurance market.

Peer reviews were provided by Mansoor Dailami (Manager, Development Prospects Group, World Bank), Caroline Freund (Chief Economist, Middle East and North Africa, World Bank), Elena Ianchovichina (Lead Economist, Middle East and North Africa, World Bank), Jean Pierre Lacombe (Head/Financial Engineering, Corporate Strategy, International Finance Corporation), Lennart Skarp (Acting Secretary General, Berne Union), Quan Li (Professor and Director of Program on International Conflict and Cooperation, Department of Political Science at Texas A&M University), Theodore H. Moran (Marcus Wallenberg Chair at the School of Foreign Service, Georgetown University), Stephen Kobrin (William H. Wurster Professor of Multinational Management at Wharton School of Business, University of Pennsylvania), and Anthony George (Ince and Co LLP).

SELECTED ABBREVIATIONS

BRIC	Brazil, Russian Federation, India, and China
BU	Berne Union
ECA	Export credit agency
EIU	Economist Intelligence Unit
FDI	Foreign direct investment
GDP	Gross domestic product
ICIEC	Islamic Corporation for the Insurance of Investments and Export Credit
ICSID	International Centre for Settlement of Investment Disputes
III	Insurance Information Institute
IMF	International Monetary Fund
MENA	Middle East and North Africa
MIGA	Multilateral Investment Guarantee Agency
MNE	Multinational enterprise
OECD	Organisation for Economic Co-operation and Development
OPIC	Overseas Private Investment Corporation
PRI	Political risk insurance
UNCTAD	United Nations Conference on Trade and Development

Dollars are current U.S. dollars unless otherwise specified.

EXECUTIVE SUMMARY

Since the summer of 2011 some of the headwinds facing the world economy have gotten stronger, resulting in downward revisions of economic growth worldwide. Within this context, the rate of growth of private financial flows into developing countries has continued to moderate after the flows' initial recovery from the financial crisis. In terms of foreign direct investment (FDI) flows in particular, there are two discernible medium-term trends that, while evident a decade ago, may be in the process of accelerating: (i) the share of FDI flowing to developing countries has continued to grow; and (ii) the share of FDI flows originating in developing countries has also continued to grow.

MIGA's 2009 *World Investment and Political Risk* report explored whether risk perceptions of the largest multinational enterprises (MNEs) based in BRIC (Brazil, Russian Federation, India, and China) countries were significantly different from those of a worldwide representative sample of MNEs. The conclusion was that risk perceptions, particularly with regard to political risk, are broadly aligned. For 2011, MIGA conducted its third international survey that measures investor risk perceptions in the short and medium term. The results for the MIGA–Economist Intelligence Unit (EIU) 2011 survey reveal an increased perception of short-term risk, but continued medium-term optimism for investment opportunities in developing countries.

In particular, short-term issues identified included heightened concerns over macroeconomic stability and difficulty in obtaining financing. Over the medium term, structural issues related to political risk remain the major preoccupations among foreign investors with operations in developing countries. Of these concerns, two stand out: breach of contractual obligations by the state and expropriatory actions (regulatory takings, creeping expropriation, and outright nationalization). These are the concerns that investors have consistently raised in the MIGA-EIU surveys when identifying key medium-term risk in developing countries. This year's *World Investment and Political Risk* report focuses on these risks.

Over the past five to 10 years, there has been an increase of expropriatory actions by governments against foreign investors, although some of this is explained by a significant increase in direct investment generally. While the nature of the expropriatory actions has changed, so that there are now more indirect expropriations—regulatory takings, creeping expropriations—than direct expropriations, even the latter have increased. Thus, MNE concerns over governmental actions that negatively affect their investment are well grounded in reality. This report seeks to analyze exogenous triggers that can lead to expropriations and how the political system intermediates disputes between host governments and foreign investors. This empirical analysis explores the triggers of disputes between governments and investors, and the conditions under which the probability of those disputes becoming expropriatory was higher. Using data from the 1970s until 2010, these were the main conclusions:

- All disputes have been triggered by an economic shock and/or significant political shift.

- In democratic regimes, the actions that initially have a negative impact are mostly taken by governmental actors other than the executive branch (for example, legislatures, and sub-national government entities), but these disputes tend to be receptive to a settlement once the executive branch is responsible for dealing with the consequences of the economic shock or political shift. It is worth noting that most political risk insurance (PRI) contracts covering expropriation have imbedded long waiting periods that permit such negotiated settlement the time to mature.

- In non-democratic regimes, the actions that initially have a negative impact are mostly taken by the executive branch, and are less likely to be resolved subsequently. Therefore, these actions become expropriations.

These findings speak to how disputes are intermediated in political regimes. In democracies, there are a greater number of players with different abilities to veto actions. Certainly, the rule of law and policy-makers' concern for their reputation and resultant re-election chances play a role. These findings are also consistent with the academic work on propensity to expropriate by regime type.

Research conducted for this report, including the MIGA-EIU survey and discussions with London-based private sector PRI underwriters and brokers, showed that the views of investors and PRI providers regarding regime type and expropriation risk differ slightly. Underwriters and brokers did not find the empirical results surprising and agreed that these results support their overall underwriting views. On the other hand, investors seemed to place a premium on stability regardless of the regime type. PRI experts also reported that it is more difficult to sell coverage in seemingly stable non-democratic regimes, as investors seem not to consider political risks that imminent. This mismatch in perception is illustrated in the Middle East and North Africa (MENA) region, where during the last 10 years PRI as a percent of total FDI seems to have been lower than the average for all developing countries. However, as events unfolded over the spring of 2011, many investors sought to get coverage at a time when private PRI providers were waiting to see how events transpired.

The third chapter of the report focuses on the PRI market and how it can support MNEs as they invest in developing countries. Rather than being driven by large-scale political events, the supply cycle in the private PRI market closely follows the trends in the broader insurance market. Over the past five years, the broader insurance industry has found itself in a situation of "soft" pricing. This has also translated into soft pricing of PRI despite the increase in demand for the product. Indeed, PRI demand has continued to increase at even faster rates than FDI growth. Over the past decades, there has been an upswing of the percentage of FDI covered by PRI, growing from a low of 5 to 8 percent in the mid-1990s to a current level of 13 to 15 percent. As a result, maximum aggregate liability has grown to historical levels. As FDI flows moderate in the short term, it may be expected that the market pricing will remain in a soft state for some time to come. Over the medium term, dynamics associated with capital requirements for banks, which are important players in this arena, may yet alter this panorama.

CHAPTER ONE

WORLD INVESTMENT TRENDS AND CORPORATE PERSPECTIVES

- The global economy is slowing down in 2011 amidst growing uncertainty and increased downside risks. Growth of private capital flows to developing countries, including foreign direct investment (FDI), is also moderating, but is expected to regain speed in the medium term.

- Developing countries now attract two-fifths of global FDI and originate close to one-fifth of overseas investment. Both shares are expected to increase given the growing importance of developing countries in the global economy, the growth differential between developed and developing counties, as well as structural characteristics and improving business environments in the latter.

- Corporate investors surveyed by MIGA—based both in the North and South—are cautiously optimistic about their investment plans in developing countries over the next 12 months, but are more optimistic over the next three years. However, they are concerned about macroeconomic stability and access to finance as potential constraints in the short term.

- Political risk remains a salient constraint to investment in developing countries, becoming more prominent over the next three years as current concerns about the global economy subside.

- The crisis in the Middle East and North Africa (MENA) region has had a negative effect on FDI, but a significant number of corporate investors surveyed have either not changed their investment plans or have adopted a "wait and see" approach. Stability is critical for persuading investors to resume investments.

Overview

Over the summer of 2011, it increasingly appeared that the rebound following the 2008 global economic crisis was losing momentum. Sovereign debt concerns in Europe, and their contagion to the banking sector, led to heightened financial volatility. The result was subdued consumption and investment in addition to strenuous fiscal consolidation measures adopted by many countries. Earlier shocks in the year, including the Japanese earthquake and tsunami and the political turmoil in the MENA region, also contributed to the slowdown. As economic growth in high-income countries remains stagnant and downside risks increase, developing countries are affected by the deteriorating global financial environment and are less likely to post the solid growth of the recent past. However, medium-term prospects for growth are favorable, showing developing countries growing at a faster pace than high-income countries.

FDI flows into developing countries, like flows into high-income economies, exhibited a sharp fall after the onset of the 2008 crisis. While they bounced back quickly, these flows to developing countries have yet to reach their peak level of 2007, and the recent downshifting of global growth is expected to weigh heavily on cross-border investment. In fact, the strong rebound of FDI to developing countries in 2010 is expected to take a slower pace in 2011. Developing countries now receive about two-fifths of global FDI, which in some measure reflects the growth differential among high-income and developing countries. Also, as developing country-based corporate investors are expanding rapidly overseas, they account for close to a fifth of total FDI.

Looking forward, the short-term outlook for cross-border investment flows to developing countries remains vulnerable to the heightened downside risks to global growth. The longer-term outlook, as viewed by global investors through the first half of 2011, augured well for sustained growth of FDI flows. Corporate investor sentiment, based on the MIGA-Economist Intelligence Unit (EIU) survey conducted in the summer of 2011 and elaborated on in this report, remains positive over the medium term—nearly three quarters of respondents have plans to expand business operations in developing countries over the next three years, and a third of them intend to do so "significantly."

In the MENA region where FDI flows had expanded rapidly during the past decade, but are expected to decline in 2011, most corporate investors seem to have adopted a "wait and see" approach, putting their investment plans on hold for now. But while investors appear willing to ride out this period of political turmoil, they are also ready to downsize their investment plans should political instability intensify and become more prolonged.

Investors' perceptions of short-term risks have worsened relative to previous years, primarily due to concerns over macroeconomic stability and access to finance. That is not to say, however, that corporate investors no longer regard political risk as an important obstacle to investing in developing countries. In fact, they continue to be particularly concerned about adverse regulatory risks and breach of contract, given the uncertainty surrounding the future regulatory landscape and regulatory responses to the current macroeconomic difficulties. Not surprisingly, the recent events in the MENA region have accentuated the risks of political violence and non-honoring of sovereign financial obligations—not only in that region, but also more broadly.

Prospects for Global Growth

The World Bank's assumptions about growth underpinning the analysis in this report depict increasing fragility and uncertainty in the face of stronger headwinds and a significant slowdown in 2011 for high-income countries (table 1.1). Developing countries have also been adversely affected: the growth assumptions also show a slowdown, raising the question of whether developing countries will be able to support a global recovery as they did in the aftermath of the 2008 crisis.

Contagion from the sovereign debt crisis in Europe has increased sovereign credit default swap rates worldwide. Sovereign debt risk perceptions have now affected overall risk appetite in capital markets and have spread beyond Europe to include a number of developing countries with close ties to the euro zone, particularly in Central and Southeast Europe. After July 2011 the cost of insuring sovereign debt (credit default swaps) increased and the Morgan Stanley Capital International emerging markets equity index declined. Private capital flows (both portfolio and FDI) into developing countries were down by 20 percent in July and August 2011. Coupled with these developments are the adverse effects of the ongoing turmoil in the MENA region, where growth, for the purpose of this analysis, is assumed to be 1.7 percent for 2011.

New challenges have emerged for developing countries. Initially, industrial production recovered and even exceeded its pre-crisis level by 20 percent. In addition, demand pressures pushed up the prices of food, energy, metals, and oil—giving rise to inflationary pressures in a number of countries. The financial turmoil that engulfed capital markets in August 2011 and the growing likelihood of another downturn dampened some of these pressures. But rising concerns about counter-party risk in the European banking system could diminish the availability of funds for short-term lending to developing countries and non-performing loans could increase in the event of a sharp slowdown in growth. Furthermore, developing countries have less fiscal space to weather another economic downturn because their response to the recession following the 2008 crisis was mainly to create fiscal stimulus. This has led to a deterioration of fiscal deficits: 42 percent of developing countries had a government deficit greater than 4 percent of GDP in 2010, versus only 18 percent in 2007, prior to the beginning of the crisis.

Prospects for Private Capital Flows to Developing Countries

Private capital flows to developing countries are still below their peak levels of 2007, although they rebounded strongly by 67 percent in 2010. For 2011, prospects for sustaining another significant increase

Table 1.1 Global Growth Assumptions*

Percent change in real GDP from previous year

	2009	2010[e]	2011[f]	2012[f]	2013[f]
World	-2.4	4.0	2.7	2.8	3.3
High-income countries	-3.8	2.9	1.6	1.8	2.2
Developing countries	1.9	7.3	6.1	5.6	6.2
East Asia and the Pacific	7.4	9.7	8.3	7.7	8.1
Europe and Central Asia	-6.5	5.2	4.9	3.8	4.2
Latin America and the Caribbean	-2.1	6.0	4.2	3.6	4.2
Middle East and North Africa	4.0	3.6	1.7	2.4	3.4
South Asia	6.2	9.1	7.0	6.8	7.9
Sub-Saharan Africa	2.0	4.8	4.9	5.3	5.6
Memo					
Developing countries excluding China and India	-1.7	5.5	4.4	3.9	4.5

Source: World Bank estimates.

Note: e=estimate; f=forecast.

* *This table reports the macroeconomic assumptions about the global economy that underpin the analysis in this report. Given the rapidly evolving global situation, actual results will almost certainly differ from these, with potentially important implications for investments in developing economies.*

are diminishing. Private capital flows (net FDI, net portfolio equity, and net debt from private creditors) are expected to remain nearly flat in 2011 on account of declines in portfolio equity flows (figure 1.1). Going forward, the pace of growth in private capital flows is expected to pick up again and exceed $1 trillion in 2013. In relation to the combined size of their economies, net private capital flows to developing countries have fallen to 4.3 percent of GDP, which is about half the share reached in the peak year 2007. That share is expected to remain around 4 percent of GDP until 2012.

Figure 1.1 Net Private Capital Flows to Developing Countries

$ billion and percent

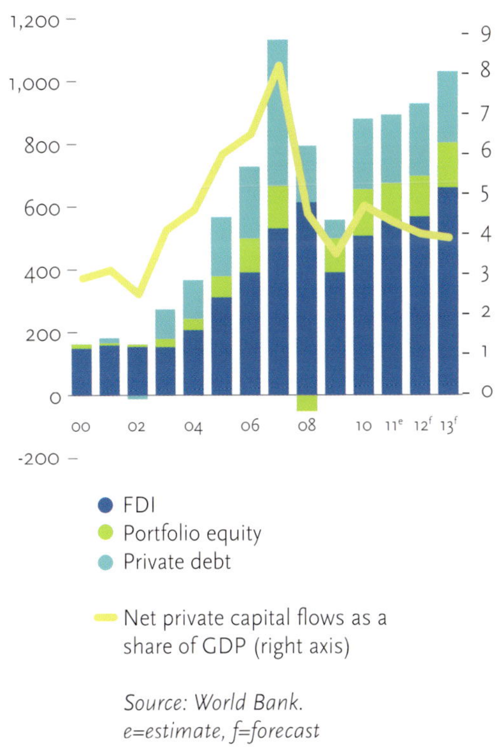

Source: World Bank.
e=estimate, f=forecast

Prospects for FDI

FDI flows worldwide, which had increased very modestly in 2010 to $1.3 trillion, are forecast to register a moderate increase in 2011 to $1.5 trillion. In the first half of 2011, the global economy continued to recover from the recession, financial and credit market conditions improved, profits increased, and multinational enterprises (MNEs) resumed their investment expansion plans. Yet, the pace of such investment is expected to moderate in the second half of the year. Cross-border mergers and acquisitions, one of the drivers of global FDI, staged a comeback in 2010 as financing constraints eased, but remain well below the previous peak of 2007. Greenfield investments, another driver of global FDI, continued to decline in value to $807 billion, also well below the 2008 peak.[1] Overall FDI flows have not returned to their pre-crisis highs of $2.3 trillion and conditions do not bode well for a significant rebound in the near future. While early signs in 2011 showed that mergers and acquisitions, as well as greenfield investments, were bouncing back, the current economic outlook could well put a brake on further growth in the second half of the year.

Mirroring their growth performances and prospects, FDI flows into developing countries increased by 30 percent in 2010 to $507 billion, a stronger rebound than previously anticipated.[2] However, a much smaller increase is expected for 2011 (figure 1.2). FDI flows to developing countries have yet to meet their pre-crisis high of $614 billion in 2008; they are forecast to exceed that level only in 2013, when FDI flows are projected to reach $660 billion. Nevertheless, developing countries once again have boosted their share of global FDI flows to almost 40 percent in 2010 and an estimated 37 percent in 2011. High economic growth (even if moderating), rising domestic demand, improving investment environments and infrastructure, and more attractive cost-productivity factors are expected to continue rendering developing countries attractive locations to both North and South-based MNEs.

The East Asia and Pacific region continues to receive the bulk of FDI flows into the developing world. With China in the lead, the region absorbed close to half of all FDI flows into developing countries in 2010 (figure 1.2). China alone, with $185 billion, accounted for 37 percent of all FDI flows into the developing world.[3] Latin America and the Caribbean were responsible for another quarter, with Brazil alone receiving $48 billion, followed by Mexico with $19 billion. In the MENA region, FDI flows fell by 7 percent in 2010 and by another 16 percent in 2011. The decline is especially evident in the sharp fall in the number of greenfield investment projects in Egypt, Libya, and Tunisia during the first four months of 2011.[4] However, a rebound is expected in 2013 as the region will generally remain attractive for foreign investors in the medium term (see the last section of this chapter). A sharp decline in FDI flows into India, which fell by 30 percent in 2010, was responsible for the steep drop in flows into South Asia in that year, but an equally sharp rebound is expected in 2011 and 2012. Led by Nigeria, FDI flows into sub-Saharan Africa are forecast to nearly double between 2011 and 2013, pushing the region's share of developing-country FDI flows from 6 to 11 percent. Exposed to the problems of the euro zone, Europe and Central Asia experienced a 10 percent decline in FDI flows in 2011.

Within this picture, FDI remains geographically concentrated in a handful of countries. Brazil, the Russian Federation, India, and China (BRIC) continue to be important investment destinations, together responsible for 60 percent of FDI flows into developing countries in 2010, a share that has increased during the past decade. A second-tier of middle-income developing countries comprising Chile, Colombia, Indonesia, Kazakhstan, Malaysia, Mexico, Peru, Turkey, and Vietnam, accounted for another fifth. On the other side of the spectrum, low-income countries received only around 3 percent of all FDI flows, a share that has remained virtually unchanged during the past decade. A group of mostly low-income economies that are also considered fragile as defined by the World Bank[5] continued to be small recipients of FDI, accounting for nearly 3 percent of the developing-country aggregate. It is important to bear in mind, however, that these low-income countries also represent a smaller share of global GDP. As was presented in MIGA's 2010 *World Investment and Political Risk* report, low-income and fragile countries receive a proportionate level of FDI flows when measured as a percentage of GDP.

MIGA-EIU Political Risk Survey 2011

MIGA commissioned its third annual survey of MNE executives worldwide to gauge investment intentions and political risk perceptions (the MIGA-EIU Political Risk Survey 2011, see appendix 2). Like the previous MIGA-EIU surveys, the 2011 survey sought to gauge the investment intentions of large MNEs vis-à-vis the developing world over the next 12 months and over the next three years. A comparison between the findings of the 2011 survey and the surveys carried out in 2010 and 2009 offers interesting insights as to how corporate investors are re-evaluating investment intentions in light of recent economic and political developments (appendix 2).

Figure 1.2 Net FDI Inflows by Developing Region

$ billion

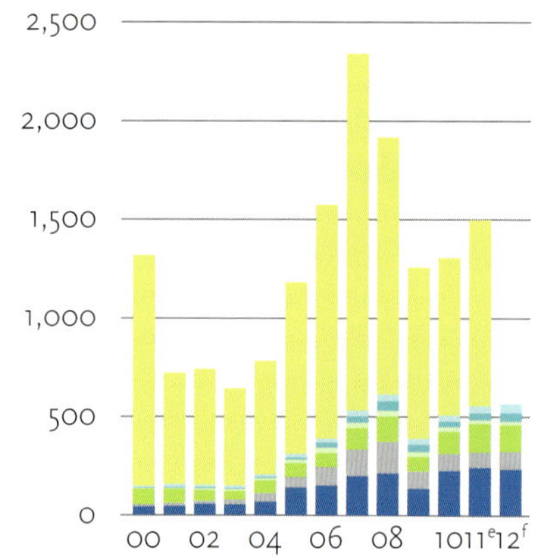

East Asia and Pacific
Europe and Central Asia
Latin America and Caribbean
Middle East and North Africa
South Asia
Sub-Saharan Africa

High-income countries

Source: World Bank.
e=estimate, f=forecast

Note: FDI inflow forecast for 2012 for high-income countries is not available.

Figure 1.3 Changes in Foreign Investment Plans

Percent of respondents

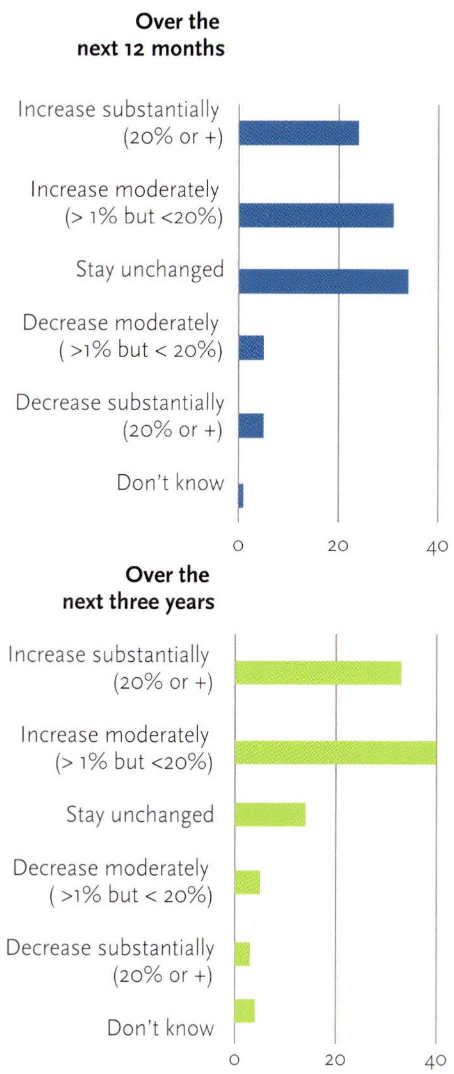

Source: MIGA-EIU Political Risk Survey 2011.

Note: Appendix 2 presents the findings for the subgroup of investors who also participated in the MIGA-EIU Survey on Political Risk in 2009 and 2010.

Figure 1.4 Changes in Foreign Investment Plans by Sector

Percent of respondents

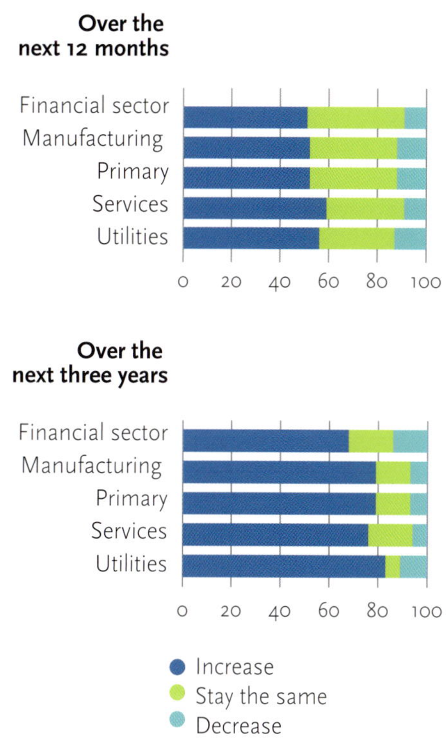

Source: MIGA-EIU Political Risk Survey 2011.

The picture emerging from the MIGA-EIU 2011 survey findings is cautiously optimistic over the near term. More than half of the respondents surveyed expect to increase their investments in developing countries over the next 12 months (figure 1.3). This is despite deteriorating economic prospects worldwide, concerns about the health of the banking sector in Europe, and fiscal austerity programs in several high-income economies. About a quarter of respondents expect to increase investments in developing countries substantially over the next 12 months, a more optimistic picture compared to the one depicted in the 2009 survey in the aftermath of the crisis. Only 10 percent of respondents in the 2011 survey planned to decrease investments in developing countries over the next 12 months, and an even lower share (8 percent) over the next three years. For the subset of respondents whose investment intentions were also tracked in the two previous surveys, this trend clearly supports the rebound in FDI flows into developing countries in 2010 and 2011 (appendix 2).

There is an important caveat: when the survey was carried out in June/July of 2011 the downside risks to the global economic growth scenario were probably not fully appraised in corporate investment plans. With that in mind, there still appears to be a clear trend of MNEs continuing to have a positive view of developing countries as investment destinations.

These findings are corroborated by other regional or country surveys. For example, Ernst & Young's 2011 Africa Attractiveness Survey of 562 international decision makers worldwide carried out in early 2011 highlighted the changing investor perspectives on Africa, especially by investors from the continent and other emerging markets.[6] The 2011 India Attractiveness Survey, also by Ernst & Young, highlighted the potential of the country's domestic market, with just over half of the 500 business leaders surveyed at the end of 2010 planning to expand existing facilities and increase operations in India, especially in states that offer business-friendly policies, fewer bureaucratic obstacles, good governance, and infrastructure.[7]

The intent of MNEs to expand operations in developing countries is prevalent across all sectors over the next three years, with only a small minority of investors anticipating a decrease in investments (figure 1.4). In comparison with the medium-term outlook, investment intentions across all sectors over the near term are less optimistic, especially for manufacturing firms.

FDI Flows from Developing Countries

After a temporary setback in 2009, net FDI outflows from developing countries were poised for another growth spurt, as MNEs from these countries resumed their global expansion plans in search of new markets and resources. In 2011, at $238 billion, the estimated value of FDI outflows from developing countries was a new record, nearly quadrupling since 2005 (figure 1.5). Developing countries now account for 17 percent of global FDI outflows, a new record share, up from 6 percent in 2005. Yet this investment, when expressed in relation to the size of their combined domestic economies (GDP), accounts on average for less than 1.3 percent—well below the corresponding ratio for high-income economies of 2 to 3 percent. This suggests a significant potential for further expansion in outward investment.[8]

FIGURE 1.5 NET FDI OUTFLOWS FROM DEVELOPING COUNTRIES

$ billion and percent

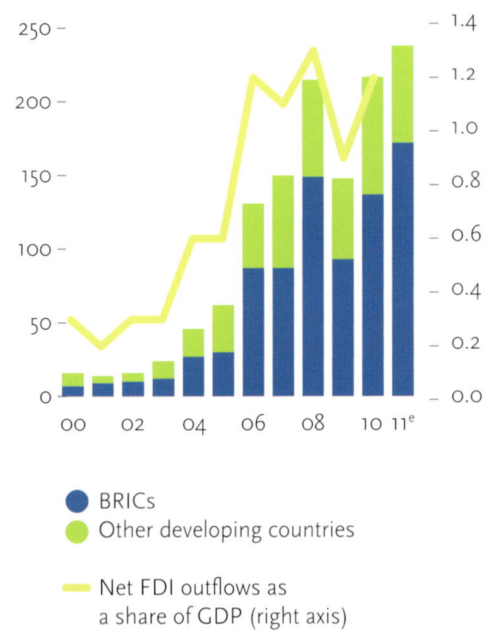

Source: World Bank.
e=estimate

As in previous years, the BRIC countries were in the lead in 2011 with $172 billion, accounting for nearly three quarters of FDI outflows from the developing world (figure 1.5). China alone invested an estimated $85 billion in 2011, a new record level, as its mostly state-owned enterprises continued their expansion into new markets and strived to become internationally competitive. Driven by acquisitions, the

Russian Federation's FDI outflows rebounded further in 2011 to $63 billion; more Russian companies are now investing overseas than foreign companies invest in the Russian Federation. India's FDI outflows also increased to $15 billion, recovering from a decline in 2010. Brazilian investment abroad, which had rebounded to $12 billion in 2010 driven by the private sector's quest for new markets and by MNEs in the extractive sector, fell to $9 billion in 2011. Motives for investing abroad vary by country: for large extractive MNEs from the Russian Federation and Brazil, the principal motive is accessing natural resources through cross-border merger and acquisitions,[9] while for Indian—and to some extent Chinese—companies, acquiring international brands is an important driver.

A second tier of developing countries with sizeable and growing investments overseas, comprising Malaysia ($15 billion), Mexico ($14 billion), Chile ($9 billion), Kazakhstan ($8 billion), Colombia ($7 billion), and Thailand ($5 billion), is following in the footsteps of the BRIC countries. Together these countries accounted for a fifth of FDI outflows from the developing world in 2010. This trend is expected to continue. A 2011 Grant Thornton survey[10] revealed that 44 percent of BRIC-based firms were considering expanding through acquisitions, compared with 27 percent in 2010. These expansions, mostly cross-border, are motivated by the desire to access new markets, resources, technologies, and brands—as well as to achieve economies of scale in production.

In the MIGA-EIU 2011 survey, South-based firms were also optimistic about prospects in the developing world (figure 1.6). Over four-fifths of the respondents indicated their intention to invest in the developing world over the next three years, further supporting the projected growth of FDI outflows. This is a somewhat more optimistic view than the one from investors based in high-income countries; however, the reverse was true for investment intentions over the short term.

Figure 1.6 Changes in Foreign Investment Plans for South-based Investors

Percent of respondents

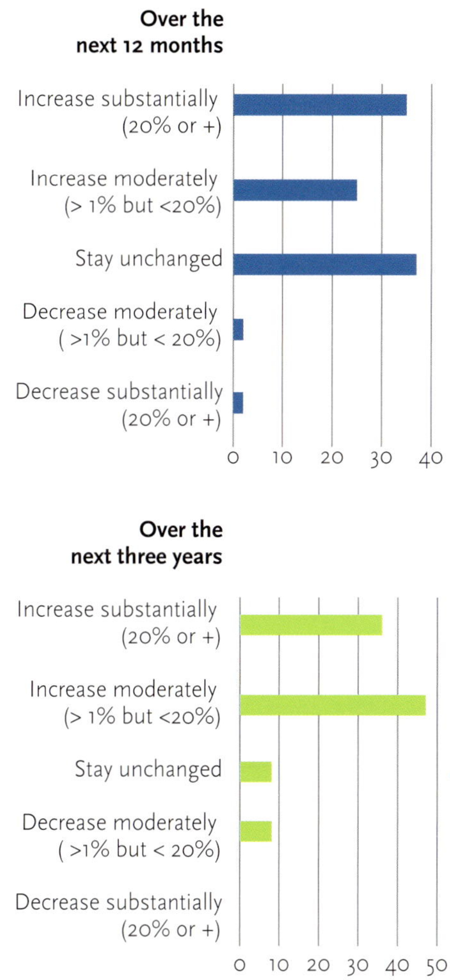

Source: MIGA-EIU Political Risk Survey 2011.

Political Risks and Developing Countries

Salient Political Risks in Developing Countries

Growing uncertainty about sustaining the global economic recovery has amplified the inherent political risks of governmental actions that affect private investors. This is illustrated by Aon's Political Risk Map 2011,[11] which shows that the level of political risk in 2011 increased in 19 countries and declined in 11. Maplecroft's Political Risk Atlas 2011[12] depicts similar trends.

Taking a closer look at specific risks, incidents of expropriation have continued to increase over the past few years (Chapter Two). Recent examples include the expropriation of a foreign utility company in Belize[13] and a copper mining company in the Democratic Republic of Congo,[14] as well as a reported 41 percent jump in the number of expropriations (domestic and foreign) in Venezuela over the previous year.[15] These expropriations, combined with elevated concerns about possible expropriations in other countries, have put this risk back at the forefront of investors' concerns. This was illustrated in the MIGA-EIU Political Risk Survey of 2010, which showed that expropriation and breach of contract registered the largest increase among political risks of most concern to foreign investors over the next three years. The MIGA-EIU 2011 survey also supported this finding, with investors perceiving the risk of expropriation to be on the rise over the next three years.

What has been termed "resource nationalism" persists as energy and extractive commodity prices remain elevated. The Fraser Institute Annual Survey of Mining Companies 2010/2011 highlighted investor uncertainty regarding the administration, interpretation, and enforcement of existing regulations as a significant deterrent to investing in a number of resource-rich developing countries such as the Democratic Republic of Congo, the Russian Federation, Venezuela, and Zimbabwe.[16] A number of developing and high-income countries have revised or are in the process of revising their mining legislation (Guinea, Brazil, Indonesia, and Australia), have raised mining taxes (royalties), or have engaged in contract renegotiations to obtain a larger share of revenues. Added to these are indigenization or empowerment requirements requiring greater local ownership and participation. For example, Zimbabwe's indigenization program requires foreign mining firms to develop and submit for approval implementation plans that require 51 percent indigenous ownership. South Africa's Black Economic Empowerment strategy requires meeting empowerment targets by 2014. In addition, foreign investors in this sector face heightened tensions arising from the distribution of royalties or tax revenues between local and central governments.

Social and environmental impacts associated with investments in certain sectors can strain relationships between investors and host-country local or central governments. In Peru, for example, the government revoked the Santa Ana mining concession of Bear Creek (Canada) following local protests about social and environmental impacts. Competition for scarce water resources can also draw attention to investments by foreign companies and shape perceptions by local populations. Maplecroft's Water Stress Index 2011,[17] a mapping of areas within countries with different gradations of water-related conflict, illustrates the potential risks facing foreign companies—especially those engaged in strategic land acquisitions—when investing in water-stressed locations.

Nearly a third of the 149 national regulatory changes introduced in 2010 that pertained to foreign investment were in the direction of increased regulation or imposing new restrictions. This compares with the results of 10 years ago, when it was estimated that only 2 percent of regulatory changes in 2000 were in the direction of increased regulation or imposing new restrictions on investments.[18] A recent report by Ernst & Young[19] that looks at overall risks facing businesses highlights regulation and compliance as the most significant threats to global firms. These include sector-specific regulatory pressures, new regulations, frequent changes in regulations, and new regulatory oversight bodies. Uncertainties surrounding the implementation of international regulations such as Basel III are also of concern to foreign investors.

Financial instability and the spectrum of heightened sovereign debt risks in high-income economies, accompanied by numerous incidents of civil disturbance and asset damage as in Greece and the United Kingdom, have accentuated political risks in high-income countries. The deep interconnectedness of high-income economies—which still account for the bulk of both inward and outward FDI—means that the transmission of these risks to other high-income economies occurs rapidly. These developments have altered perceptions of political risks being specific to developing countries alone.

Figure 1.7 Ranking of the Most Important Constraints for FDI in Developing Countries

Percent of respondents

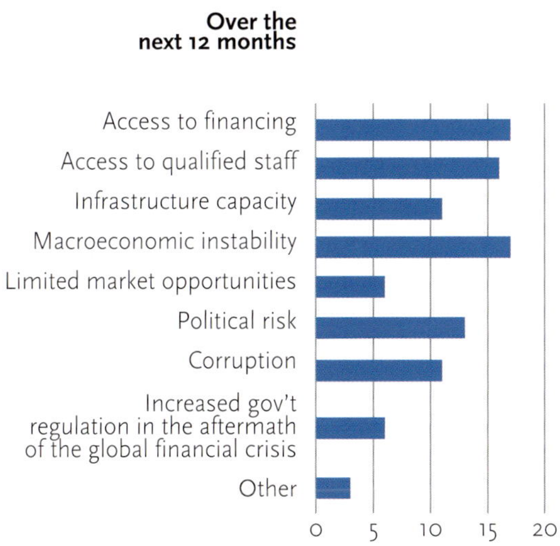

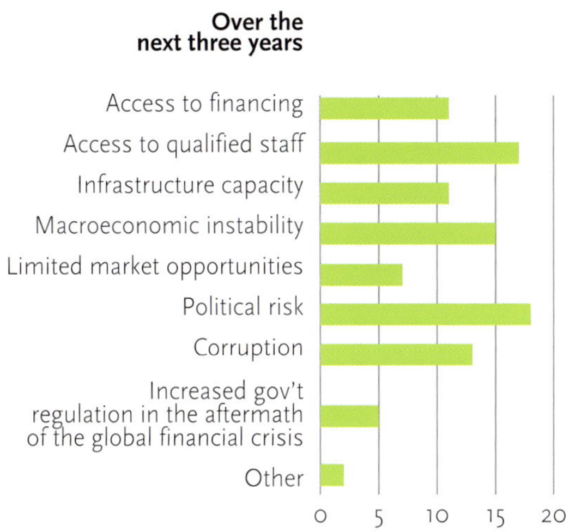

Source: MIGA-EIU Political Risk Survey 2011.

The growing interdependence of the global economy also means that production disruptions owing to political risk events occurring in one country may have negative effects that extend beyond national boundaries. As global outsourcing, just-in-time production, and international production supply chains multiply, so does the risk of disruption from political events. Certain industries—such as automobile, electronics, and the extractives sector—that depend on closely interconnected but globally located production networks, are particularly susceptible. The cost of such disruptions can be significant for MNEs: for example, the 2011 earthquake and tsunami in Japan—although not a political risk, but a significant supply chain disruption—caused an estimated $200 million a day in losses in the automobile industry alone.[20]

A recent survey[21] on risks and supply-chain disruptions highlighted the significance of risk assessment in the supplier-selection process. In selecting suppliers, almost 90 percent of respondents claimed to consider some form of risk assessment, with companies taking steps to evaluate the supplier's exposure to a variety of risks, including geopolitical risks. Despite this high rate, one of the survey's conclusions was that often companies are not well prepared to respond to supply-chain disruptions and are not proactively managing this risk.

Poor governance continues to plague many countries around the world and poses enhanced reputational and integrity risks. To some extent, heightened attention through legislation to these issues by a number of countries that are sources of FDI in the developing world—for example, the Foreign Corrupt Practices Act in the United States and the Bribery Act in the United Kingdom—help to reduce such risks. In addition, more countries adhere to conventions addressing bribery adopted by the United Nations, the European Commission, and the Organisation for Economic Co-operation and Development (OECD).[22] Yet, as of August 2011, only 12 countries are validated as compliant with the Extractive Industries Transparency Initiative;[23] certainly governance and transparency are vital to the extractives sector.

Corporate Perceptions of Political Risk in Developing Countries

All of the above concerns have resulted in investors' heightened perceptions of political risk in recent years.[24] This was also confirmed by the MIGA-EIU 2011 survey, in which political risk was ranked as corporate investors' top concern over the next three years for MNEs based in both developing and high-income countries (see box 1.1 for the definition of political risk).

Figure 1.8 Types of Political risk of most Concern to Investors in Developing Countries

Percent of respondents

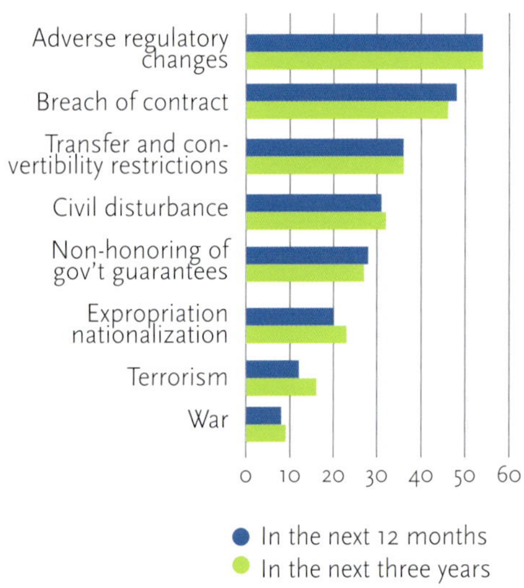

Source: MIGA-EIU Political Risk Survey 2011.
Note: Percentages add up to more than 100 percent because of multiple selections.

Three years since the onset of the global economic crisis, the growing fragility of the global economy and the return of elevated downside risks have placed macroeconomic instability at the forefront of investor perceptions of constraints to FDI (figure 1.7). In the MIGA-EIU 2011 survey (appendix 2), foreign investors ranked macroeconomic instability as their chief concern over the next 12 months, followed by access to financing. This is not surprising given the delicate economic situation in high-income countries where most investment originates. The state of the global economy is perceived as a significant and growing constraint to investment plans in developing countries also for the subgroup of investors who participated in the earlier MIGA-EIU surveys on political risk (see appendix 2). Despite the weak state of the global economy taking precedence over the next 12 months, pushing political risk down in the rankings, political risk nevertheless remains one of the most important concerns for investors. Over the medium term, as concerns about the economy subside, political risk once again rises in investors' perceptions as a significant obstacle to FDI, ranked among their top three concerns.

Figure 1.9 Types of Political Risk and their Effects on the Company

Percent of respondents

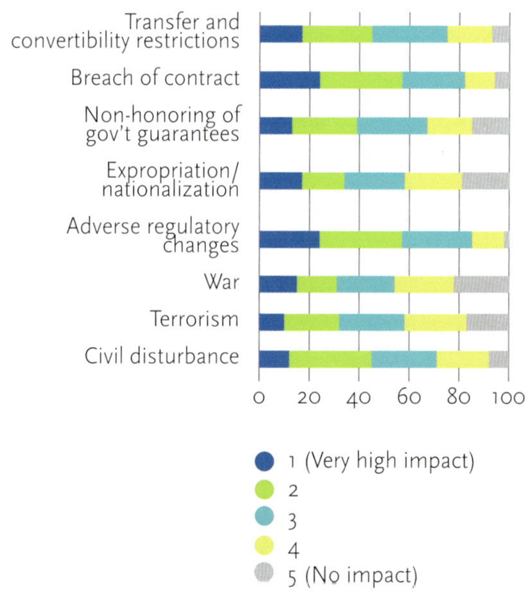

Source: MIGA-EIU Political Risk Survey 2011.

Concerns about political risk are particularly high for South-based investors.[25] South-based investors are also concerned about macroeconomic instability and limited access to financing in the short term, but the majority of them see political risk as the biggest constraint to their investment plans over the medium term. This is in contrast with North-based investors, for whom macroeconomic instability remains the principal concern in both the short and medium term.

Regulatory risks (adverse regulatory changes) ranked first among concerns in the MIGA-EIU 2011 survey over the next 12 months and over the next three years, surpassing breach of contract as the political risk most vexing to investors (figure 1.8). The importance of regulatory risk is a finding that has been consistently supported in both the 2009 and 2010 surveys, underscoring the weight that investors place on risks posed by regulatory uncertainty and "market-unfriendly" changes in laws and regulations in host countries. Difficulties in predicting future regulatory changes also render investors less able to assess how such changes might affect the value of

Box 1.1 Definition of Political Risk

Political risk broadly defined is the probability of disruption of the operations of companies by political forces and events, whether they occur in host countries or result from changes in the international environment. In host countries, political risk is largely determined by uncertainty over the actions not only of governments and political institutions, but also of minority groups and separatist movements.

For the purposes of the MIGA-EIU Political Risk Survey, the definition of political risk includes the following:

- **Transfer and convertibility restrictions**: risk of losses arising from an investor's inability to convert local currency into foreign exchange for transfer outside the host country. Currency devaluation is not covered.
- **Expropriation**: the loss of investment as a result of discriminatory acts by any branch of the government that may reduce or eliminate ownership, control, or rights to the investment either as a result of a single action or through an accumulation of acts by the government.
- **Breach of contract**: risk of losses arising from the host government's breach or repudiation of a contractual agreement with the investor, including non-honoring of arbitral awards.
- **Non-honoring of sovereign financial obligations**: risk of losses due to non-compliance of government guarantees securing full and timely repayment of a debt that is being used to finance the development of a new project or the enhancement of an existing project.
- **Terrorism**: risk of losses due to politically motivated acts of violence by non-state groups.
- **War**: risk of losses due to the destruction, disappearance, or physical damage as a result of organized internal or external conflicts.
- **Civil disturbance**: risk of losses due to social unrest.
- **Other adverse regulatory changes**: risk of losses for foreign investors stemming from arbitrary changes to regulations.

the future income streams and investment in general. Discussions with investors point to the instability of the regulatory regime as the key concern, rather than the regulatory regime itself. Especially for investors in the financial sector, regulatory changes have increased in the aftermath of the global financial crisis, as host-country governments have considered a range of possible interventions, in particular to regulate foreign banks and other financial institutions.

The United Nations Conference on Trade and Development (UNCTAD), World Trade Organization and OECD, which have been tasked by the G-20 to track such measures, have concluded that host-country governments have not instituted permanent protectionist measures in response to the crisis. In the organizations' latest joint report,[26] they note that the majority of G-20 countries have eliminated most restrictions on international investment put in place during the financial crisis.

Figure 1.10 Proportion of Firms that Have Suffered Losses as a Result of Political Risk over the Past Three Years

Percent of respondents

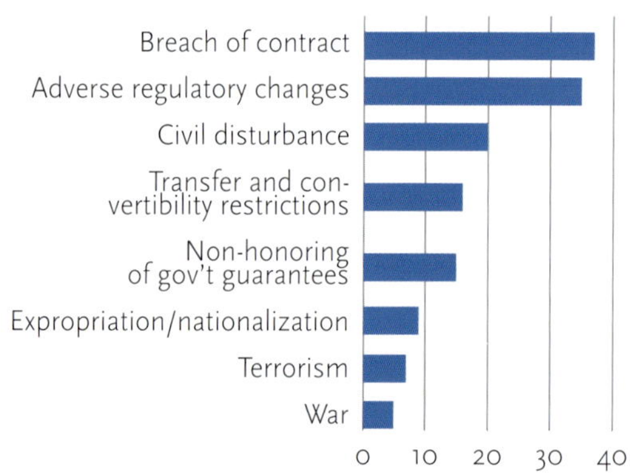

Source: MIGA-EIU Political Risk Survey 2011.
Note: Percentages add up to more than 100 percent because of multiple selections.

Figure 1.11 Proportion of Firms that Have Withdrawn or Canceled Investment Plans on Account of Political Risk over the past 12 Months

Percent of respondents

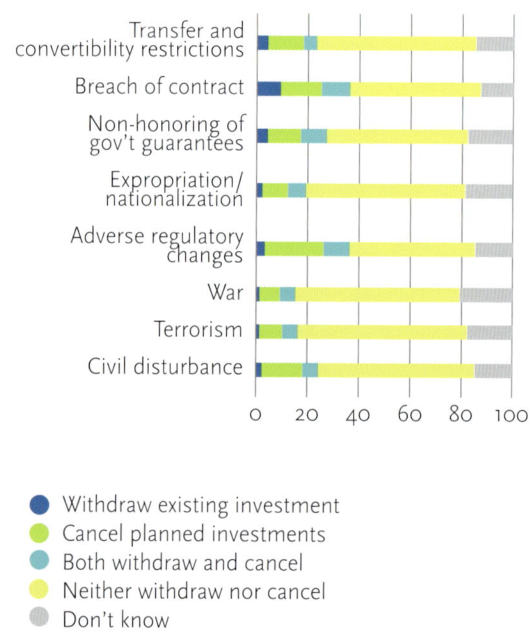

Source: MIGA-EIU Political Risk Survey 2011.

Foreign investors' concerns with increased adverse government regulation may be validated by national policies introduced in response to the 2008 crisis as governments sought to protect key industries or proposed international regulations, such as Basel III. However, with regard to FDI, and in contrast to trends in international trade, host governments have now largely unraveled whatever temporary policies were put in place in response to the crisis.

Political risks can create significant adverse effects on the operations of MNEs. Consistent with this, adverse government regulation and breach of contract were the two risks perceived to have the biggest negative effects on foreign investments (figure 1.9). Political violence risks, especially war and terrorism and to a lesser extent civil disturbance, did not rank high in terms of negative effects. In fact, a sizeable proportion of respondents claimed they were completely unaffected by the presence of these risks in the developing countries where they operated. These finding are consistent with losses actually experienced by investors as a result of different political risks (figure 1.10). Breach of contract and adverse regulatory changes, political risks that investors face frequently in host countries, were also the risks for which investors claimed the most losses over the past three years.

In general, political risks are not perceived to be very high in the countries where MNEs operate; however, they do have an impact on investments. In particular, adverse regulatory changes and contract breaches forced a significant minority of investors to withdraw or cancel existing or planned investments (figure 1.11). These findings are in line with those of previous surveys. However, the majority of respondents have not experienced political risk in a way that has caused them to take any action.

Spotlight on the Middle East and North Africa

Despite the overall positive attitudes regarding corporate investment intentions in developing countries, the recent unexpected turmoil in the MENA region[27] has affected FDI plans there. The turmoil led to disruptions in economic activity, plummeting tourism and FDI flows, all of which have negatively affected economic growth (table 1.1). In Egypt, the economy shrank by 4.2 percent on an annualized basis during the last quarter of 2010 and the first half of 2011,[28] while in Tunisia the decline in the first quarter of 2011 from the previous quarter was 3.3 percent on an annualized basis.[29] For developing countries in the MENA region, estimates for 2011 have been revised downwards.[30]

This broadly painted picture of the MENA region masks important differences across individual countries. Such differences were also present in the pattern of FDI prior to the onset of the recent upheaval. When considering both high-income and developing countries in the region, Saudi Arabia emerges as the biggest recipient of FDI in terms of both flows (figure 1.12) and stocks—but such investment is comparatively less significant in relation to the size of its economy than in smaller countries like Lebanon. The United Arab Emirates and Saudi Arabia have also been the biggest sources of FDI in terms of both flows and stocks. Among only developing MENA countries, Libya and Egypt, both of which were significantly affected by recent events, had been the biggest investors overseas.

Figure 1.12 Cumulative FDI Flows in MENA, 2000-2010

$ billion

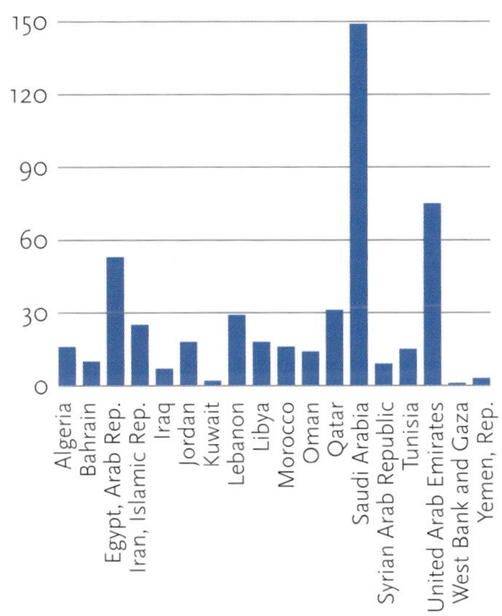

Source: World Bank.

High-income oil exporters in the MENA region receive the bulk of FDI flows overall. Subdividing developing MENA countries into oil-exporting and oil-importing economies produces an even more polarized picture (figure 1.13). Up until the early part of the past decade, FDI flows into all of these groups were relatively small, fairly equivalent in size, and growing slowly at similar rates. Toward the middle of the past decade, the growth of FDI flows into high-income oil exporters, such as Saudi Arabia and the United Arab Emirates, accelerated rapidly, while flows into developing-country oil exporters like Algeria, Iran, and Libya increased more slowly. Developing-country oil importers, in particular Egypt and Tunisia, saw a significant increase in FDI compared with the developing-country oil exporters.

Figure 1.13 FDI Flows into MENA

$ million

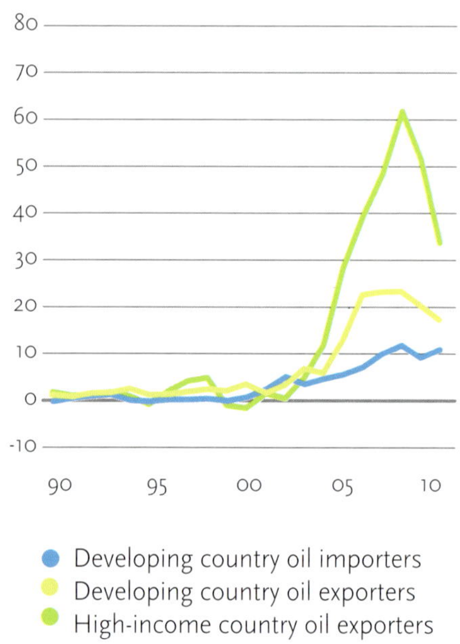

Source: World Bank.

The financial crisis of 2008 led to declines in FDI flows into the MENA region, and as political events unfolded in 2011, the flows plummeted further in the countries directly affected. In the first quarter of 2011, FDI inflows turned negative in both Egypt and Tunisia,[31] while greenfield investments in Egypt declined by 80 percent in the first four months of 2011 compared with the same period in 2010.[32]

Prospects will depend on the speed of resolving the political situation, since investment takes longer to recover than economic growth.[33] The World Bank has forecast that FDI flows into the MENA region will decline in 2011 and 2012, but it expects them to grow again in 2013. Over the medium and longer term, economic and demographic factors—a combined population of 450 million people, 90 million of whom are between the ages of 15 and 25[34]—will continue to attract market-seeking foreign investors, even more so under conditions of improved governance and less cumbersome frameworks for doing business.

Figure 1.14 Current Regional Distribution of FDI in Selected MENA Countries

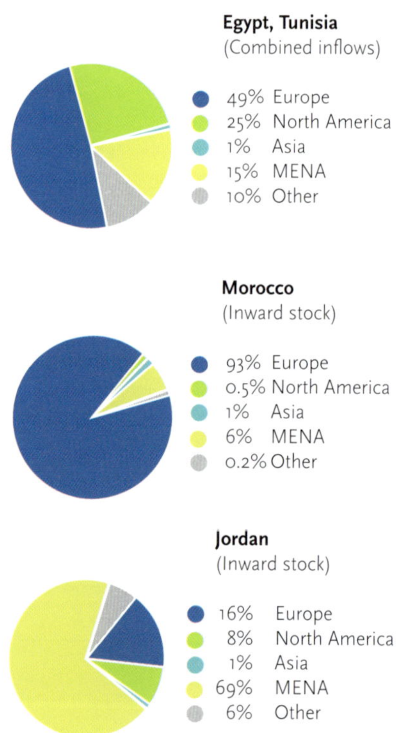

Source: IMF, Coordinated Direct Investment Survey Database and national sources.

Traditionally MENA countries have been mostly reliant on MNEs either from other countries in the region (both high income and developing) and Europe. With strong trade relations[35] with the European Union and historical ties, Europe has been a big investor in Egypt and Tunisia, accounting for around half of those countries' combined FDI flows, and for virtually all of Morocco's FDI received since independence (figure 1.14). But for other countries in the region, intra-MENA investment has been responsible for most of their FDI: as of 2009, over two-thirds of Jordan's stock of FDI originated from countries within the region (figure 1.14).

Figure 1.15 Effect of the Recent Turmoil in MENA on Investment Plans in the Region

Percent of respondents

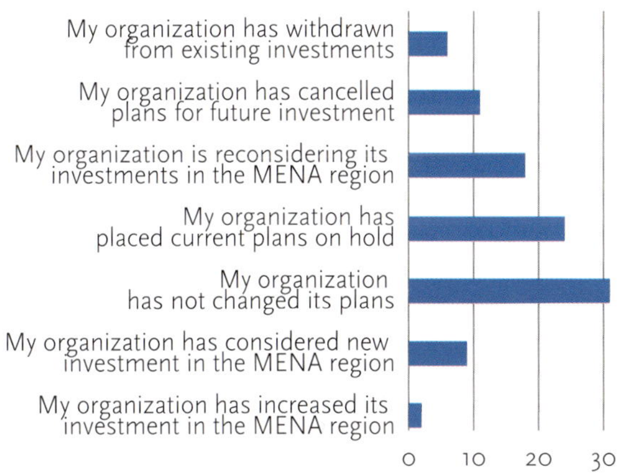

Source: MIGA-EIU Political Risk Survey 2011.

These patterns are likely to affect FDI prospects. Despite recent announcements of investment intentions in North Africa by other countries in MENA,[36] short-term prospects are not promising. With Europe under economic strain and uncertainties surrounding the political environment of Egypt, Libya, and Tunisia, FDI into North Africa is likely to slump for longer and rebound more slowly than the rest of the MENA region.

Figure 1.16 Effect of the Recent Turmoil in MENA on Political Risk Perceptions in the Region by Type of Risk

Percent of respondents

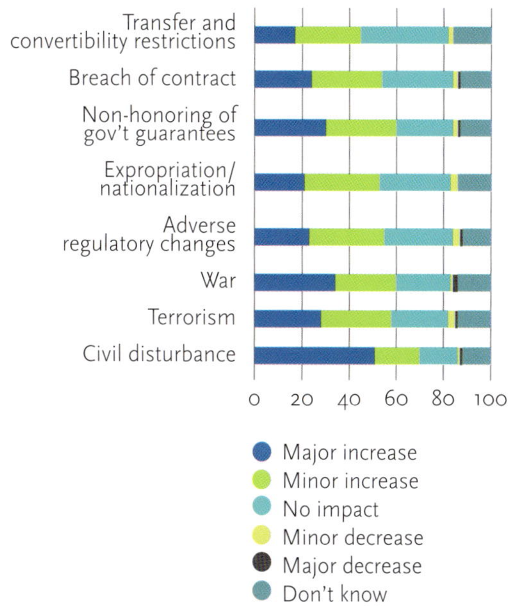

Source: MIGA-EIU Political Risk Survey 2011.

In the context of developments this year, with turmoil still present and a great deal of uncertainty over ongoing political changes, it is not surprising that a recent survey by Grant Thornton[37] found that over one-fifth of the privately-owned companies participating disclosed that the events in the MENA region have had a negative impact on their business. The positive side was that despite these events, only one-tenth of the companies surveyed expressed a reduced likelihood of doing business there. This finding suggests that despite the recent turmoil, the longer term outlook for the region remains promising and companies do not view the present unrest as posing a long-term barrier to doing business in that region.

Figure 1.17 Effect of Regime and Stability on Investment Plans in the MENA Region

Percent of respondents

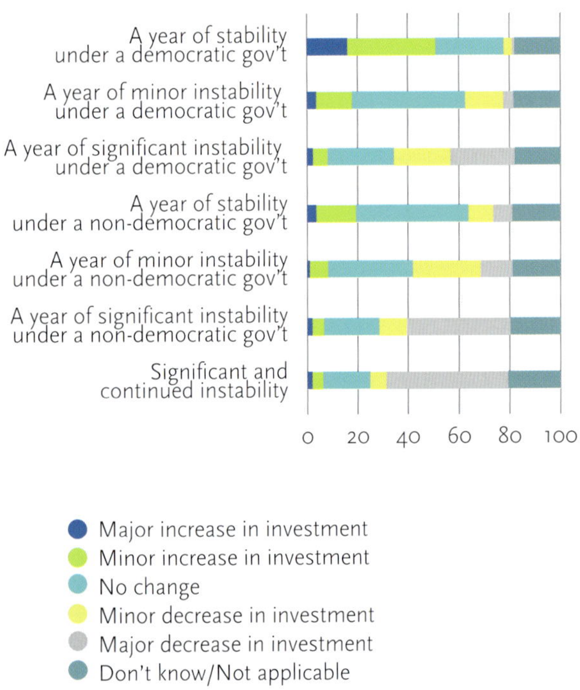

Source: MIGA-EIU Political Risk Survey 2011.

The findings of the MIGA-EIU 2011 survey, which questioned corporate investors worldwide on their investment intentions in the MENA region, largely reflect the same sentiment. The turmoil did have a significant impact on investment intentions—the majority of investors who had existing investments or plans to invest in MENA put their plans on hold, reconsidered, canceled, or withdrew their existing investments (figure 1.15). A higher proportion of firms withdrew existing investments or canceled investment plans compared with the proportion of firms that increased investments or considered new investments in that region. However, just below a third of firms did not alter their investment plans. Despite heterogeneity among the different countries in the MENA region, on balance, the turmoil has stressed existing investments and dampened plans for expansion or new investments. Some existing investors in the countries directly affected by the unrest, especially in the energy sector, have reported suspending operations (for example, ConocoPhillips, Hess Corp., Marathon Oil, and Occidental Petroleum in Libya).[38] MNEs in the service sectors, especially tourism, have also reported reduced activity. All of this has been amplified by the worsening state of domestic economies, as current account balances and budget deficits widened, private capital flows weakened, inflation rose, and production and investment declined.

Political violence (especially civil disturbance and to a lesser extent war and terrorism) ranked particularly high as the risk of most concern to foreign investors (figure 1.16) in the MENA region. Investors have also been concerned about governments' ability to honor their sovereign financial obligations in light of increased sovereign risk, rising sovereign credit default risk spreads, and foreign currency sovereign debt rating downgrades.

Investors were also surveyed on their attitudes on stability and regime type (an element that will be detailed in Chapter Two). Just over half of the firms appeared ready to invest in the MENA region assuming there is at least a year of stability under a democratic government (figure 1.17). The stability factor, however, is not to be underestimated. Nearly half of these firms said they would decrease investments should there be significant instability, even in the presence of a democratically elected government. Only 8 percent of these firms would increase their investments under such circumstances. The worst-case scenario from investors' point of view would be prolonged and significant instability, in which case nearly half of the firms would decrease investments substantially. Some 44 percent of the firms surveyed claimed that they would not change their plans for investment, essentially adopting a "wait and see" approach in the event of a non-democratic regime that nevertheless succeeds in stabilizing the country for at least a year.

Figure 1.18 Effect of the Recent Turmoil in MENA on Investment Plans in Developing Countries in Other Regions

Percent of respondents

Source: MIGA-EIU Political Risk Survey 2011.
Note: Percentages add up to more than 100 percent because of multiple selections.

The turmoil in the MENA region has not significantly affected investment intentions in other developing regions. Political global contagion appears to have been contained. This is also manifested in the findings of the MIGA-EIU 2011 survey, in which nearly half of the respondents had no intention of making any changes to their investment plans in other regions (figure 1.18) as a result of events in MENA countries. However, for a significant minority (about a tenth of respondents), the MENA events did lead to withdrawal or cancellation of investments in other developing regions.

Despite growing uncertainties and an increasing likelihood of a negative economic scenario, foreign investors remain optimistic about prospects in developing countries, as reflected in their investment plans, especially over the next three years. While political risk remains an important concern as a constraint to investment, economic instability has gained prominence in the near term. In the MENA region, there has been an adverse effect on investment intentions arising from the recent turmoil. The longer term implications are uncertain and not favorable should instability persist. Investment plans in other developing countries have not been affected significantly by the events in the MENA region.

CHAPTER TWO

GOVERNMENT TAKINGS AND EXPROPRIATIONS

- The probability of disputes between governments and foreign investors is materially increased by an economic shock and/or significant political shift.
- Not all disputes between governments and foreign investors result in expropriatory action; this outcome is heavily influenced by the regime type of the host country.
- In democratic regimes, expropriatory actions are mostly taken by governmental actors other than the executive branch. They also are likely to be settled because of institutional characteristics such as rule of law, checks and balances of power, multiple players with veto power, and the importance of reputation to policymakers.
- While using different data sources, MIGA's analysis corroborates recent academic literature on propensity to expropriate by regime types.

Overview

The uncertainty arising from potential governmental intervention in private investments is consistently cited by investors as a key risk factor in many developing countries. This chapter examines the conditions under which government intervention is more or less likely to occur. The empirical analysis of this issue used two data sources: one contains incidences of conflict between an investor and a host government with a wide array of outcomes, including expropriation, and another only contains instances of actual governmental expropriations. The analysis tests earlier academic research[39] that questions whether the type of the political regime—democratic vs. non-democratic—makes a difference in the propensity to expropriate in the context of an economic shock requiring a public policy response.

Analysis shows that, while economic crises are highly correlated with disputes between investors and host governments, expropriations themselves are not specifically correlated with these crises. Something else triggers the dispute to become an expropriation: the political regime. Democratic regimes are less likely, all things being equal, to engage in expropriatory behavior compared with non-democratic regimes. The apparent reason is a cost-benefit analysis where the benefit is the asset acquired from a private investor, and the cost is the loss of reputation and consequent future decrease in investments. It appears that a democracy, with checks and balances, rule of law, and policymakers concerned with their reputations as they face elections, is more careful in its behavior when dealing with property rights. Thus, there is a lower probability of expropriations.

However, investors do not seem to completely appreciate this effect. In fact, they seem to value political stability over regime type partly because expropriation, even in a high-risk environment, is a low-probability event. Investors also seem to view the risk in hindsight rather than foresight, which reinforces the value attached to past stability in political regimes.

Risk of Government Interference in Private Investments

A risk that foreign and domestic investors typically face is the intervention of governments in their operations in such a way as to constitute a taking or an expropriation of their assets, rights to operate, or ability to continue an operation. In the past two years, MIGA has published *World Investment and Political Risk* reports, which have included the surveys discussed in Chapter One of this report. In these surveys, investors consistently maintain that governmental interference and expropriation of foreign direct investment (FDI) is one of the key risks that concern them. This year's report presents the same finding.

Expropriation of foreign investments has been a recurring risk for a long time. In exploring this topic, the questions investors may be most interested in are: What motivates governments to expropriate? What can investors do to understand this motivation and mitigate against it? Have anything been learned from recent history?

This chapter seeks to understand the motivations of interference in investment from the host government's point of view. A useful way to look at expropriation risk is illustrated in recent academic literature that maintains that the government's decision to expropriate has a benefit (control of the assets that can be used for productive purposes) and a cost (loss of reputation that will lead other investors not to select the country as a recipient for their funds).[40] The analysis explores why expropriations do not, in fact, occur more frequently—given that the costs are generally intangible and are in the future, yet the benefits are tangible and immediate. As the state is not a single rational actor, but a series of actors with different pressures and incentives, the cost-benefit calculation becomes potentially more complex. For this reason, the regime type and the existence of few or many actors within it are critical elements in understanding expropriation risk.

Recent Trends in Expropriation

The frequency and nature of expropriation events relating to FDI has changed over time. During the 1960s and 1970s, acts of expropriation came about in response to political risks centered largely on post-colonial declarations of independence, civil wars, and left-wing takeovers—whether through elections or coups d'état. Newly formed governments confiscated or nationalized foreign investors' property under the argument that this would herald the end of exploitation and the start of national sovereignty. Estimates put the number of expropriation acts during 1960-1979 at 560.[41] During that time estimates show that 15-20 percent of the volume of all U.S. FDI abroad measured in volume terms was nationalized.

This picture changed in the second half of the 1970s when the number of expropriation acts dropped dramatically,[42] in part because most of the vulnerable assets had already been confiscated.[43] In the 1980s and up until the early 1990s, new expropriation acts diminished markedly. During 1980-1986, estimates of the number of expropriation acts declined to 16.[44] During this time, more liberal economic policies were taking root in a number of developing countries, and expropriations were associated with the learning curve of initial efforts to enact new regulatory frameworks, hesitant reforms, and backsliding. By the early 1990s, when efforts to liberalize, privatize, and deregulate economies were in full swing, there was a sense that expropriations were a thing of the past as governments implemented national foreign investment regimes and participated in international investment treaties.

Since 1995, backlash against these liberalizing policies, accompanied by incomplete deregulation of domestic markets and transitions in political systems, led to a higher incidence of expropriation cases, especially in Latin America and Central and Eastern Europe. A recent estimate places the number of expropriation acts during 1996-2006 at 41, with 15 occurring during the period 1996-2000 and 26 occurring during the period 2001-2006.[45] The value of expropriated assets during 1990-2006, estimated using data from arbitration claims, accounts for 1.6 percent of developing countries' FDI stock, compared with 4.4 percent during 1960-1976.[46]

Figure 2.1 Expropriation Acts by Sector

Number

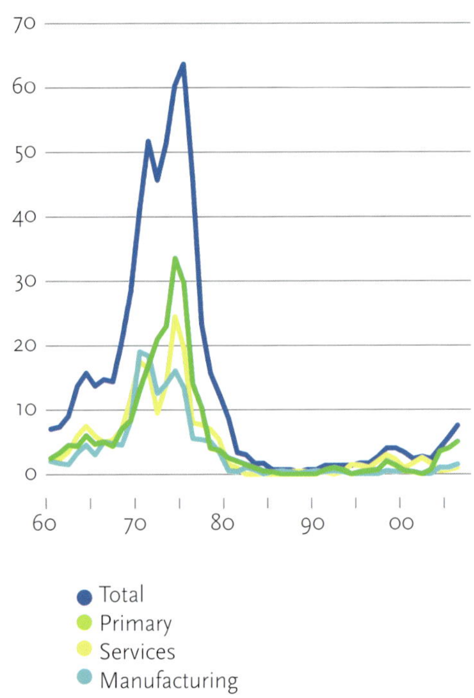

Source: Chris Hajzler (2010), "Expropriation of Foreign Direct Investments: Sectoral Patterns from 1993 to 2006," University of Otago.

The primary sector has seen the largest spike in expropriation acts (figure 2.1). Most developing countries use royalties or income taxes, as opposed to production-sharing arrangements, to draw revenues from foreign-owned mining projects. This has not always been satisfactory to host governments. Public utilities have also been affected by host governments reneging on commitments. This has arisen either from popular pressures—as in the case of the Cochabamba, Bolivia water concession in 2000; some governments seeking to retain popular support—as in the case of Argentina over the past decade; or the inability of governments to abide by commitments made as part of an incomplete reform process—as in the case of the Dominican Republic's energy sector in the early 2000s.

The nature of expropriatory acts by governments also changed from the direct expropriations (outright nationalizations) that were seen in the 1960s to the indirect or "creeping" expropriation acts of the last few years. Despite this trend, outright confiscations still occur. Moreover, as mentioned in Chapter One, they have been on the rise in the past few years.

Expropriation[47]

Under what circumstances is the risk of government interference in private investment increased? While most governmental interventions in private investment are characterized by idiosyncratic factors, some broad risk characteristics can be discerned from available data on expropriations and other governmental interventions into private investments. Here, a more critical and less anecdotal treatment of this risk both for the political risk insurance (PRI) industry as well as for foreign investors is warranted. The data come from Berne Union (BU) institutions, as well as from the International Centre for the Settlement of Investment Disputes (ICSID). The BU is an association of export-credit and investment insurance agencies most of which are public institutions from developed countries (for example, the Overseas Private Investment Corporation of the United States, Export Development Corporation of Canada, Coface of France)—though a handful of private insurance firms are also represented (see box 3.1). ICSID, whose secretariat is part of the World Bank Group, is an arbitration forum for disputes between host-country governments and foreign investors.

Data from these organizations have important differences: the BU identifies expropriation claims paid[48] and ICSID identifies disputes that may or may not have resulted in the need for the state to indemnify a private firm. This difference is critical because expropriation decisions may best be explained as a two-step process: the governmental action itself and the subsequent negotiation that either compensates foreign investors or results in an insurer paying for the loss.

For the purpose of this analysis, data of actual expropriations and disputes were tabulated from various sources. A regression analysis was then used to discover whether a series of variables could explain a higher probability of disputes or expropriation. The tested variables related to characteristics of political regimes (democratic vs. non-democratic), the actors within the state (for example, executive branch, legislative branch, sub-national), as well as changes in economic and political conditions.

Before outlining the results of the findings, a couple of clarifications are needed. In the empirical analysis a number of existing measures of democracy are used, but for the sake of discussion a democratic regime is defined as one in which the opposition has a reasonable prospect of achieving political power in the absence of violence. Non-democratic regimes are defined as the contrary. In the analysis, the political regime type was defined as binary, notwithstanding the reality of shades of gray between the two extremes.

A second clarification regarding economic shocks is that they do not only have to be negative. The recent upsurge of resource nationalism is, in fact, an example of a positive shock—as commodity prices increase, the incentive of the government to take over these assets also increases. For the analysis, what matters is a material change in economic conditions.

This analysis shows that the risk of expropriatory actions by the state increases in the aftermath of major political or economic change. In the last 20 years there has been no case of an expropriation that has not been preceded, in a narrow or a broad sense, by a political or economic shock. For example, 23 high-profile expropriations of U.S. investments were the result of major political transitions such as regime change in Iran after the fall of the Shah, or major economic crises that triggered political change. In some cases it is difficult to establish whether an economic crisis triggered the political crisis. But it is clear that major political shocks impact a government's choice to expropriate.

The nature of the economic crisis does not seem to matter; financial, fiscal, or debt crises all can result in an enhanced probability of expropriatory action. This may seem intuitive as expropriatory actions tend to result from the public policy discontinuities that crises may bring. The key issue is that an economic crisis leads to actions by the government that affect—intentionally or not—private investments in the country. This pattern is very clear in the ICSID data, where investment disputes are much more common in periods of economic crisis.

It is clear that major political or economic changes can increase the risk of expropriation, but what other factors are at play? Since governmental interference has to go through the public administration, the nature of the political regime also has an influence. Research has explored the different dimensions of democracy, ranging from free and fair elections, the ability of voters to participate in elections, mechanisms to allow true competition between individuals and parties, and constraints on the executive after an individual wins office. Taking into account these multiple dimensions of democracy, research shows clear divisions in the tendency to expropriate based on the type of political regime:

- In democratic regimes, the actions that initially have a negative impact are mostly taken by governmental actors other than the executive branch—such as legislatures, or sub-national entities of government. But the resulting disputes tend to be settled—either with or without explicit mediation—once the executive branch is responsible for dealing with the consequences of the economic shock or political shift. In fact, most PRI contracts covering expropriation have embedded long waiting periods that can give a negotiated settlement the time to mature.

- In non-democratic regimes, the actions that initially have a negative impact are mostly taken by the executive branch of government and are less likely to be resolved. Therefore, these actions become expropriations.

- Expropriations occur in both democratic and non-democratic regimes, but the propensity to expropriate is significantly higher in non-democratic regimes.[49]

These conclusions derive from the statistical analysis of the two different data sets. First, the correlation between economic or political crisis and investment disputes was tested using ICSID data. These data refer only to the existence of a dispute, not necessarily its outcome. A significant correlation indicates that in the aftermath of an economic or political crisis public policy discontinuities lead to increased disputes between investors and governments. However, when the same analysis was carried out with data of actual expropriations (as opposed to disputes), there is no significant correlation. This indicates that the hypothesis of economic or political crises leading to disputes holds, but that there is something that is more closely correlated to expropriation. This is the political regime type.

The general perception is that the rule of law is stronger in democratic regimes than in non-democratic ones and permits more scope for legal redress to wronged investors. But the analysis also suggests another rationale. If governmental actions to expropriate result from the cost-benefit analysis described earlier, where the benefit is access to assets and the cost is a loss of reputation, then the cost will be greater for policymakers who have to face electorates. This loss of reputation may exist with respect to both domestic and external audiences. The linkages between the two, however, appear to be stronger in democratic regimes than in non-democratic regimes. Therefore, in democratic regimes there is a combination of policymaker incentives and multiple actors with power to redress acting together to strengthen the consistency of decisions over time. The final result is a decrease in expropriation events. Box 2.1 explores the experience of Indonesia in 1997-98 that illustrates this hypothesis.

Other factors can affect the cost-benefit calculation of expropriation and will be addressed in future research. For example, countries rich in natural resources may be less concerned about reputational issues. Alternatively, countries that are dependent on foreign aid are especially concerned about their reputation since adverse actions against investors not only affect private investment flows, but also potentially can affect the flow of foreign aid.

Risk Perceptions of Foreign Investors in Developing Countries

In the MIGA-EIU 2011 survey, most international investors view disputes as arising from actions by the executive branch of government, either directly or indirectly. Yet, in a separate analysis of expropriation and arbitration claims, the role of the executive is most pronounced in non-democratic regimes. In democratic regimes, many disputes initiate from sub-national governments or regulatory agencies. To restate, not all expropriatory actions are initiated by the executive; in fact, in democratic regimes, usually the executive is initially not involved.

Figure 2.2 Independence of Agencies when Acting Against Investors

Percent of respondents

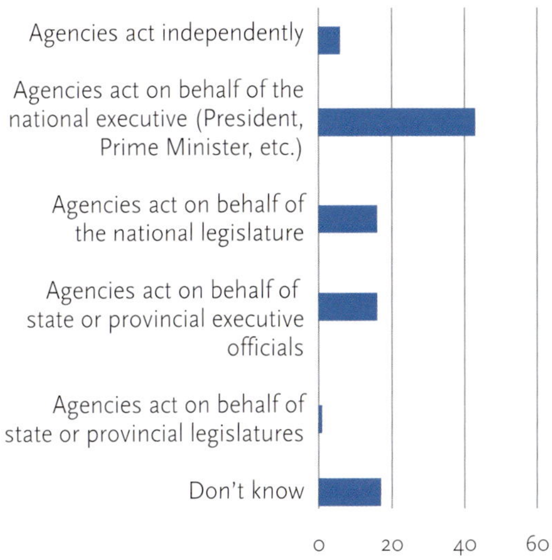

Source: MIGA-EIU Political Risk Survey 2011.

The results are interesting when the survey questions turn to types of governmental regime. There is a strong perception that democratic regimes mitigate the risk of expropriation due to checks and balances, rule of law, incentives, and consistent behavior by policymakers. However, results regarding perceptions of non-democratic regimes are inconclusive. Investors recognize the value of rule of law, but are not as keenly aware of the risks associated with the absence of democracy. The key risk identified is corruption—which is not associated with a particular regime type, and is often associated instead with a country's level of development.

Finally, when asked to identify key drivers of expropriation, the single most important response is the existence of a prior uncompensated expropriation. This is important and understood intuitively by policymakers. It is the key reason why policymakers in democratic regimes understand that their reputation will suffer and costs will be incurred as a result of expropriation.

Figure 2.3 Political Regime and its Impact on Business Decisions

Percent of respondents

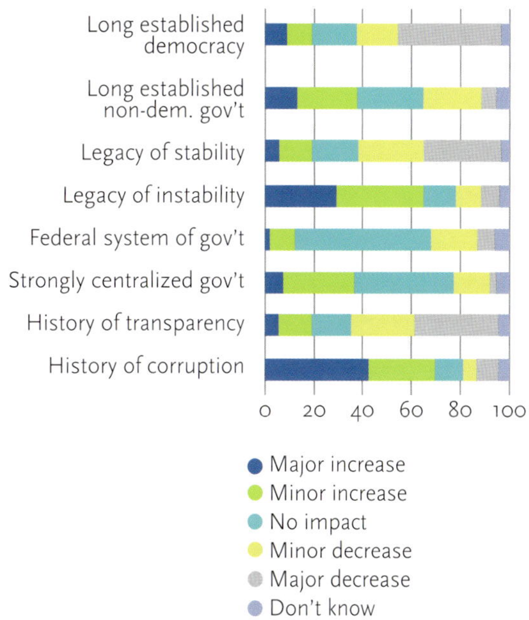

Source: MIGA-EIU Political Risk Survey 2011.

Reputational effects are an important factor in assessing the results. While expropriations may dramatically lower investment, the political consequences of this lack of investment can vary. For example, entrenched leaders in non-democratic regimes may be able to weather the political backlash caused by the reduction in FDI. Parties of the left and

Box 2.1 Indonesia in 1997: A Case Study that Underscores the Research Results

Since the 1970s, Indonesia experienced stable and rapid GDP growth at an average of 7 percent annually, raising per capita income toward the level of middle-income countries. Sovereign risk spreads had been at a low level prior to the Asian financial crisis, which reflected the stable market perception of the Indonesian economy. On the other hand, the economy was highly centralized under Suharto's "New Order" regime, which masked the structural weakness of the economy. Business opportunities were concentrated to politically connected parties, such as the president's family and relatives. Under this regime, Indonesia's investment climate suffered in comparison with other ASEAN countries. Concerns included uncertain business operation, excessive regulation, and corrupt transactions.

Following the currency turmoil in Southeast Asia in July 1997, Indonesia faced the greatest economic instability among neighboring countries: real GDP declined by more than 10 percent, the rupiah depreciated by 80 percent, and inflation rose to above 60 percent. The crisis not only adversely affected the economy, but also further worsened the social and political environment of the country. World Bank governance indicators confirm the sharp decline in the business environment and the quality of government after the crisis. The deterioration of governance indicator scores relating to rule of law, regulatory quality, government effectiveness, and control of corruption reflect the political turmoil and the increase in expropriation after the 1997 crisis.

In this context, two documented cases of expropriation targeted assets held by foreign investors in utility industries in 1998. The crisis severely affected private power projects in Indonesia—long-term power purchasing agreements with private power producers seriously suffered from the increased threat of contract defaults and renegotiations.

This demonstrates that economic crisis can trigger expropriation, especially in a non-democratic regime like pre-crisis Indonesia. As indicated by the negative score of the rule-of-law governance indicator, there were few players to veto the expropriatory actions by the executive branch of the Indonesian government. In the recession that followed the crisis, the government placed a higher value on resources and was tempted to expropriate private assets out of desperation—even though this resulted in the loss of reputation, a worsened business climate, and a huge drop in foreign investment. The economic and political turmoil resulted in the resignation of Suharto, followed by the liberalization of the economy, and democratization under the supervision of a three-year stand-by arrangement by the International Monetary Fund.

Sources:

- *The World Bank. 1998. "The East Asian Financial Crisis – Fallout for Private Power Projects." Public Policy for the Private Sector Note No. 146.*
- *Kaufmann, Kraay, and Mastruzzi. 2004 "Governance Matters III: Governance Indicators for 1996, 1998, 2000, and 2002."* The World Bank Economic Review.
- *IMF. 1998. "Financial Market Contagion in the Asian Crisis." IMF working paper 98/155.*
- *Hajzler, Chris. 2010. "Expropriation of Foreign Direct Investments: Sectoral Patterns from 1993 to 2006." University of Otago, Economics Discussion Paper No. 1011.*
- *Asian Development Bank. 2005. "Improving the Investment Climate in Indonesia." Asian Development Bank: Manila.*
- *Michael Tomz and Mark Wright. 2010. "Sovereign Theft: Theory and Evidence about Default and Expropriation." In* The Natural Resource Trap: Private Investment without Public Commitment, *ed. William Hogan and Federico Sturzenegger. Cambridge, MA: MIT Press*

right may also be impacted differently, based on how their core supporters value foreign investment and how supportive they are of expropriation.

Investors responding to questions about how different political and economic changes affect political risk said that financial crises rank among the biggest drivers. In addition, most investors viewed potential political change as increasing risk. Yet, while a shift to a left-wing government had a modest increase in political risk perception (37 percent of respondents said it led to a "minor increase"), a shift to a populist government saw a much more dramatic increase.

Risk Perceptions of Investors and PRI Providers

The analysis shows clear evidence that economic crises and political regime type play a major role in increasing the probability of expropriations. An interesting characteristic of expropriation risk is that the risk itself has a relatively low probability—but very high severity. In that sense it is an infrequent, yet catastrophic, risk. Thus, while there are factors that may substantially increase the probability of expropriation, the one-year expropriation probability remains relatively low compared to the probability of other adverse corporate events. This means that corporate decision makers will not experience many expropriation claims in their professional careers, if they experience any at all. This leads to a certain degree of over-confidence in the ability to predict and manage the risk. PRI providers, by contrast, see more expropriation events—actual or potential—as they are covering a wide array of firms, industries, and countries.

This difference in perception leaves MNEs exposed to risk. According to the survey, investors appear more concerned about stability than about regime type and political institutions in general. And the most important factor that will impact an MNE's decision whether to move forward with an investment is the existence of uncompensated expropriations in the country being considered. This may be useful for potential new entrants, but is too late for those already present in that country, indicating investors would benefit from considering additional elements in their decisions that are more forward-looking.

Figure 2.4 Factors that Investors Perceive as Increasing Risk

Percent of respondents

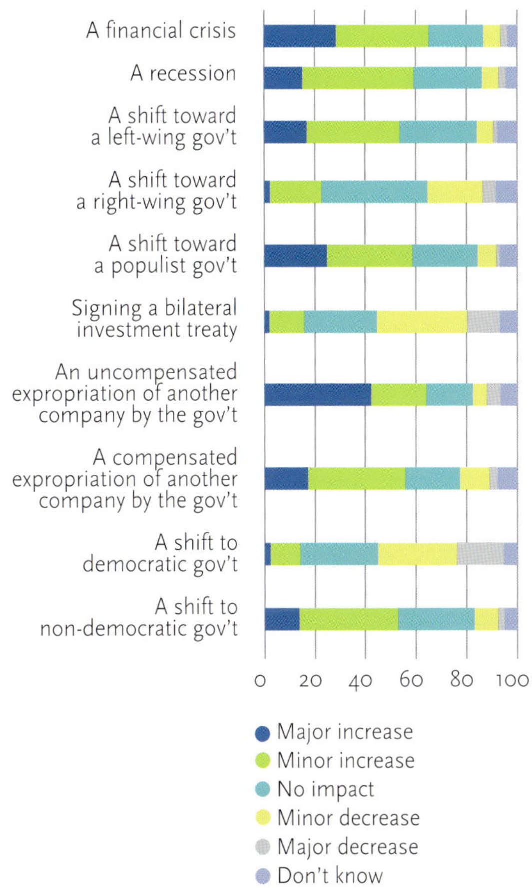

Source: MIGA-EIU Political Risk Survey 2011.

CHAPTER THREE

THE POLITICAL RISK INSURANCE INDUSTRY

- Demand for political risk insurance (PRI) is on the rise. Heightened global risk perceptions in the aftermath of the global financial crisis, further fueled by sovereign credit risk in the developed world and political crises such as the Arab Spring, have led to unprecedented levels of demand for the product.

- High demand for PRI was reflected in a sharp uptick in new investment insurance issued by Berne Union members since 2008. 2010 marked a record year for the industry. In the first half of 2011 this trend appears to be continuing, although downside risks have started to emerge from a weakening of Europe's banking sector.

- PRI supply remains abundant and pricing reflects a buyer's market. Mirroring the now longest period of a "soft" supply cycle in the general (non-life) insurance industry, the private PRI market appears robust and well-positioned to meet the high demand for the product.

Overview

The first months of 2011 were a reminder of the unique risks that foreign investors face in emerging markets. Côte d'Ivoire experienced months of turmoil after a contested presidential election in November 2010, which ultimately led to an armed and prolonged standoff. Food-price inflation, a long-term ill affecting countries suffering from demographic pressures and simultaneous nutrition shortages, has led to social unrest in Bolivia, Burkina Faso, Mauritania, Mozambique, Uganda, and other countries. In North Africa, social uprisings arising from dissatisfaction with public mismanagement and corruption led to the removal of long-established rulers. The salience of political risk in the broader context of emerging-market risk is consistently mirrored in this and past editions of the MIGA-EIU survey on political risk.

Heightened political risk perceptions are reflected in a marked increase in issuance of PRI. In 2010, the Berne Union (BU) insurers (box 3.1) reported a record $65.8 billion in new underwriting, up approximately 30 percent over 2009. Similarly, private market underwriters and brokers report an all-time high demand for insurance against political risk. PRI issuance has grown, not only in absolute terms, but also relative to foreign direct investment (FDI). Over the past five years, the rate of growth of PRI has exceeded that of FDI, meaning that a higher percentage of FDI is now insured for political risk. In 2011, this trend appears to be continuing as new business written by BU members between January and July remained brisk. However, higher capital requirements and a weakening of Europe's banking sector could potentially slow new business in the second half of 2011 if financing becomes scarcer.

Commensurate with this increase in new business in 2010, premium revenues reported by BU members increased to $1.16 billion, a 15 percent increase over 2009. Loss ratios in PRI are more difficult to measure historically. Investment insurance claims paid by BU members in 2010 spiked to $221 million, a tenfold increase over 2009, leading to a markedly higher aggregate loss ratio of 20.5 percent. However, single-year loss ratios are sensitive to single-event data points and may not give an adequate picture of industry-combined ratios, especially when losses are smoothed over time. Overall, the PRI industry remains well capitalized and the trend of further "softening" of premium rates continued well into 2011.

Most significantly, political risk was brought to the fore in what came to be known as the Arab Spring. The Arab world shares a variety of economic woes and there is certainly no shortage of social pressure points that governments will have to address across the region, as discussed earlier in this report. A common shortcoming in many of these countries is that the private sector has been insufficiently harnessed as an engine for job creation, social development, and economic growth. Some economies, particularly those that are not large oil producers, also lagged behind other regions' levels of foreign investment and private capital formation. This means they have often fallen short of what is necessary for an effective process of economic modernization.

For the PRI industry, the significance of the Arab Spring is twofold. First, it demonstrates how sudden and unexpectedly political order can erode in changing societies. For investors, PRI can serve as an effective hedge against the risks of sudden political disruption, and already the industry has begun to see a significant increase in demand for its products. Second, the PRI industry can play an important role in restoring investor confidence in the region. As MENA countries stabilize in the medium term, attracting foreign capital will be paramount and PRI providers can support foreign investors in tapping the region's potential.

The PRI industry in 2011 – Trends and Prospects

The high volume of new investment insurance issued by BU members in 2010 marks the continuation of a longer-term trend of rising demand for PRI. During the 1990s new PRI cover provided by political risk insurers was nearly flat, and actually decreased slightly in real terms. Measured as a ratio to annual FDI flows into developing countries, PRI underwriting declined from 25 percent in the mid-1980s to a low point of nearly 5 percent in 1997.

At the end of the 1990s, the declining real demand for PRI gradually reversed. More private political risk insurers entered the market to compete with, and offer coinsurance alongside, public insurers. Capacity in the market surged with the entry of new private insurers and the increased competition among providers of PRI led to an increasingly dynamic product-innovation environment. As a result, PRI products have adapted to the changing needs in the marketplace, both by increasing the scope of coverage as well as developing very specialized subcategories of insurance.

Coverage against political violence, for example, was made available for a greater number of contingencies including political riots, demonstrations, civil disturbance, insurrections, and terrorism—with policies being able to approach coverage selection with more flexibility. Terrorism insurance itself became a primary catastrophe insurance product after the events of September 11, 2001 in the United States, although it is generally offered in the property/casualty market. More recently, non-payment insurance on financial obligations from sovereign obligors and contract frustration/non-payment cover have become the fastest growing products in the PRI market.

Box 3.1 The Berne Union

The Berne Union (BU) was founded in 1934 with the mandate to promote international acceptance of sound principles in export credit and investment insurance. Today, the BU has 78 members (including Prague Club members[a]) comprising mainly export credit agencies (ECAs), multilaterals, and private insurers (appendix 2). Most ECAs and multilaterals are BU members, as are a smaller number of commercial insurers including Chartis (formerly AIG), Zurich, and Sovereign Risk Insurance. In October 2008, Hiscox became the first private insurer underwriting in Lloyd's to join the BU. In 2010, ECAs accounted for about 79 percent of the BU's outstanding investment PRI portfolio, private members accounted for 19 percent, and multilaterals accounted for 5 percent.

The BU plays an important role in bringing together the public and private insurers to enhance cooperation and information sharing. Members meet on a regular basis to discuss industry trends and challenges. In recent years, there has been a concerted effort on the part of the BU secretariat to promote transparency and disclosure in the industry and to represent member interests in order to encourage global trade and investment.

---

[a] The Berne Union's Prague Club was started in 1993 with funding from the European Bank for Reconstruction and Development. It is an information exchange network for new and maturing insurers of export credit and investment. The Prague Club supports members' efforts to develop their export credit and investment insurance facilities by hosting technical discussions at twice-yearly meetings, as well as ad-hoc information exchanges. A number of Prague Club members have gone on to meet the requirement for full BU membership.

FIGURE 3.1 PRI AND FOREIGN DIRECT INVESTMENT FLOWS INTO DEVELOPING COUNTRIES

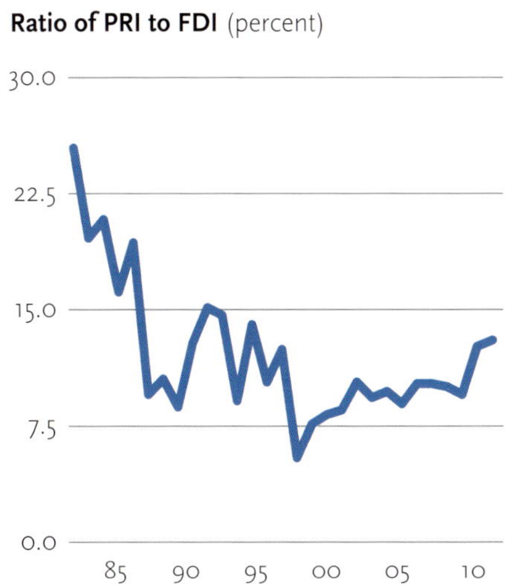

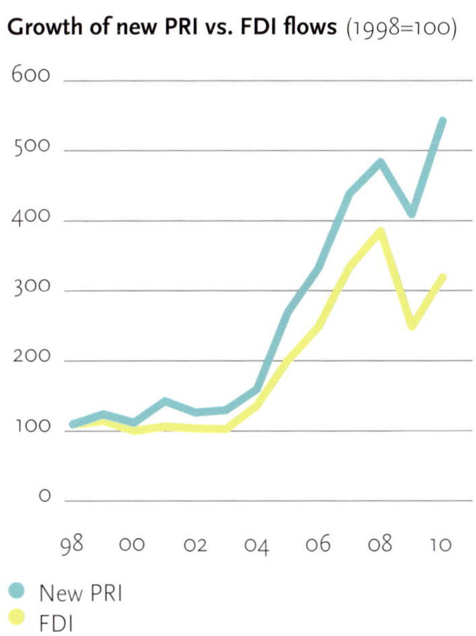

Source: Berne Union Secretariat and World Bank.
Note: Investment insurance data for 2010 cannot readily be compared with previous years' data due to a new classification of this business.

The trend toward enhanced supply of PRI through product innovation and the growing financial capacity of market players occurred alongside rising demand, driven primarily by increased global FDI flows. Since 2000, investment flows into developing countries nearly quadrupled from $160 billion in 2000 to $580 billion in 2008 (a annual growth rate of 17.5 percent). The surge of FDI flows into developing countries since 2000 gave support to a very rapid growth of PRI issuance over the last decade, which occurred at even higher rates of growth than FDI. New investment insurance cover provided by BU members grew even more rapidly from $12.7 billion in 2000 to $66 billion in 2010, representing an annual growth rate of 18.6 percent. Consequently, the ratio of PRI to FDI in developing countries increased to 14 percent in 2010—the highest level since the early 1990s (figure 3.1).

However, the ratio of FDI and PRI issuance differs significantly across developing-country regions. Proportionally, most PRI is issued for investments in Africa. Between 2005 and 2010, the average ratio of FDI to PRI for sub-Saharan Africa was 18 percent. In Latin America and the Caribbean, the corresponding ratio was 12 percent, followed by Eastern Europe and Central Asia (10 percent), the Middle East and North Africa (9 percent), and Asia (6 percent).

In the wake of the global financial crisis, developing-country FDI fell sharply in 2009 and rebounded only partially thereafter. New PRI coverage also declined during the crisis, but only slightly. The amount of new business underwritten by BU members in 2009 was only marginally lower than in 2007, the year prior to the financial crisis. While nominally PRI business did not grow during the crisis, it remained stable in relative terms. Measured as a ratio to FDI flows into developing countries, PRI increased from 9 percent in 2008 to 13 percent in 2010. In absolute terms, new business in 2010 was up about 34 percent over 2009, or around 12 percent over its peak level in 2008. The swift recovery of PRI issuance is particularly striking in North America and Western Europe, which remain the primary markets for PRI even though FDI flows today are still around 50 percent below pre-crisis levels.[50]

The speedy recovery of the PRI market since the financial crisis of 2008 mirrors the prominence of political risk in an environment of heightened global risk aversion. Since MIGA launched its annual political risk survey in 2009, political risk has featured consistently among the highest-ranked constraints to FDI in emerging markets. This year, events sur-

Box 3.2 Overview of the PRI market

The PRI market includes three broad categories of providers and covers both export or trade credit and investment insurance. For the purposes of this report, PRI refers to investment insurance. The public PRI market comprises both national and multilateral PRI providers. The private market's PRI falls into two main categories: (i) political risk activities similar to that of the public insurers, such as coverage for investments in emerging markets against expropriation, political violence, and other such risks; and (ii) emerging market non-payment insurance covering contract frustration and default by governments.

The National PRI Providers: These include national export credit agencies and investment insurance entities. They focus on cross-border trade and investment, generally for constituents in their own countries.

The Multilaterals: These include the African Trade Insurance Agency, the Asian Development Bank, the Inter-American Development Bank, the Inter-Arab Investment Guarantee Corporation, the Islamic Corporation for the Insurance of Investment and Export Credit, and the Multilateral Investment Guarantee Agency. The World Bank, the Asian Development Bank, and the Inter-American Development Bank also provide risk mitigation instruments, such as partial risk guarantees.[a]

The Private PRI Market: The majority of private insurers are based in three insurance centers—London, Bermuda, and the United States (primarily New York City). Several of the larger insurers have offices in Singapore; Hong Kong SAR, China; Sydney; and elsewhere. As well as traditional equity PRI, the private market offers protection for a wide variety of developing-country payment risks, either for political perils alone or comprehensive non-payment cover. Brokers play an important role in promoting and sourcing PRI for the private market. This market segment is dynamic: over the past year, some players have exited the PRI market, while new entrants have appeared.

The Reinsurers: Reinsurance companies underwrite PRI-related coverage for both trade and investment. Reinsurance is an underlying factor driving both pricing and capacity in the private market. Some of the top reinsurers include Munich Re and Hannover Re of Germany, Swiss Re of Switzerland, and Berkshire Hathaway/General Re of the United States. Export credit agencies and multilaterals also participate as reinsurers of PRI, although on a smaller scale.

---

[a] A partial risk guarantee covers private lenders against the risk of government failure to honor contractual obligations relating to private projects.

Source: Data on national providers from Berne Union and on private providers from Arthur J. Gallagher & Co., London.

rounding the Arab Spring, election uncertainty in a number of still nascent democracies, and popular unrest following exorbitant food price inflation have further underscored the salience of political risk. In the broader context of uncertainty over the future of the euro zone, the long-term fiscal health of high-income economies, and anemic growth of the global economy, developing-country risk aversion is likely to remain elevated for some time to come.

High demand for PRI is observed by a number of market participants. Marsh insurance brokers reported an unprecedented level of demand for PRI in its 2011 mid-year market update.[51] Similarly, the African Trade Insurance Agency reported that "the demand for political risk insurance surged in light of increased debt protection costs and yields on government debt across the Gulf region"[52] and Lloyd's underwriters speak of the biggest upsurge in business since September 11, 2001.[53] MIGA has received a continuously growing number of inquiries for political risk guarantees since the onset of the financial crisis. Guarantee applications received by MIGA in 2011 increased by 15 percent over 2010, following a 34 percent increase in the previous year.

Pricing and Capacity

Despite a global environment of heightened risk aversion and increased demand for the product, for now the PRI market remains "soft". Premium rates remain subdued and capacity is widely available. As a Lloyd's broker noted recently, the PRI market in London continues to be robust. The market had a difficult patch when a wave of claims came through as the financial crisis hit the real economy after the failure of AIG. While these losses primarily hit the trade finance side of the business, they indirectly affected the investment side through reserves required by insurers. As a large fraction of the private PRI business covers comprehensive non-payment insurance, with much of this issuance covering obligations from private sector obligors, one could expect that losses would have caused underwriters to withdraw from the market, resulting in a reduction of market capacity. But there is no evidence that the financial crisis had that effect. A Lloyd's underwriter commented on the continued robustness of the market, explaining that not only were the financial crisis-related claims dealt with very efficiently, but in addition, the private market capacity increased over the period that included the crisis.

In the private PRI market, pricing continued to soften throughout 2011. According to London-based broker RFIB, pricing for specific country coverages quoted by Lloyd's and company underwriters has either remained stable or decreased since January 2011, both in the investment insurance and the sovereign non-payment segments of the market. The exception to this trend is the MENA region where non-payment pricing increased for a small number of sovereign borrowers including Algeria, Egypt, Syria, and Yemen.

Figure 3.2 Ratio of Premiums to Average PRI Exposure for BU Members

Percent of insured amount

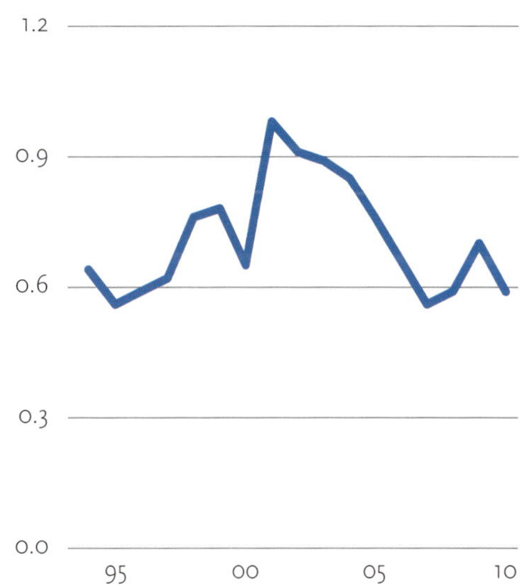

Source: Berne Union Secretariat.

Pricing reported by BU members rose somewhat in the aftermath of the financial crisis in 2008. Figure 3.2 shows the ratio of annual premium income to average outstanding liabilities reported by BU members. While this remains an imprecise measure of prevailing price levels, this ratio gives a rough estimate of how premium income from new contracts compares to income under expiring contracts. The ratio was at its lowest level at 0.56 percent in 2007, before it increased to 0.7 percent in 2009 as new contracts were booked at proportionally higher premium rates. In 2010, the premium level stabilized at 0.58 percent.

Figure 3.3 Available Private Market PRI Capacity

$ million

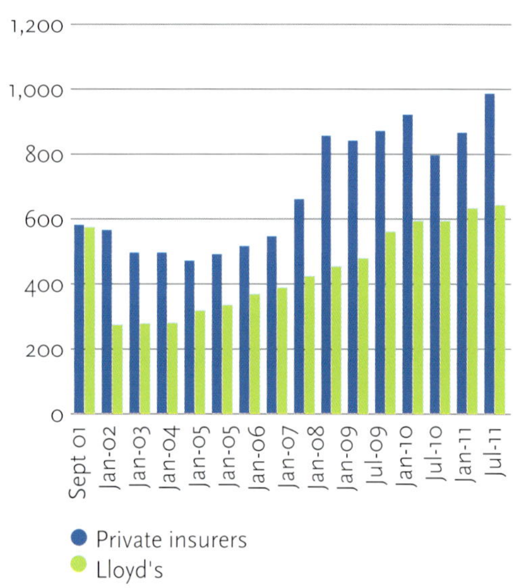

Source: Arthur J. Gallagher & Co.

Brokers report that the Arab Spring so far has produced a relatively small number of claims in the investment insurance segment of the market. Trade credit losses did arise in several MENA countries, but risk exposure in the region has traditionally been small. Several brokers report a large number of trade credit claims in Libya and estimate that total losses resulting from the Libyan conflict could amount to $300-500 million. However, so far it appears that most of those potential claims have not translated into losses for insurers. PRI exposure in the MENA region is relatively small: BU members' liabilities in Egypt, Libya, Tunisia, Syria, and Yemen account for only about 5 percent of global outstanding insurance contracts (also see figure 3.7).

In terms of capacity, the PRI industry appears to be well positioned to respond to the ongoing rise in demand for PRI. Arthur J. Gallagher & Co. brokers estimate in their July 2011 market update[54] that capacity in the private market has increased by almost 25 percent since July 2010 (see figure 3.3). Lloyd's capacity also increased, though by a smaller degree—8 percent. According to market reports, single providers have tended to increase available line sizes and tenors, indicating that the industry continues to have solid risk appetite—contrary to the apparent general increase in risk aversion among international investors. Overall, the increase in insurance capacity reported in July 2011 continues a long-term trend. The 2009 exit of a major player in the industry, Chubb Insurance—which at the time accounted for the reduction in capacity in 2010—has been more than compensated over the past year by expanded capacity of remaining members and some new participants.

The PRI Cycle and the General Insurance Market

The persistence of the soft PRI market is not an isolated phenomenon. Market conditions in the broader general insurance market are equally soft and liquid. Insurance broker Marsh notes that in the first half of 2011, the multinational insurance market continued to experience softening across some global property and all international casualty segments. Indeed, the commercial side of the PRI industry appears to closely mirror the conditions of the general insurance market. To the extent that PRI is often managed as a specialty line by general insurance companies, liquidity and pricing correlate with the general insurance market. As the PRI portfolio is dwarfed by that of general insurance, the PRI supply cycle is not idiosyncratic, but closely follows trends in the general insurance cycle.

Figure 3.4 illustrates how PRI market capacity and general insurance pricing have trended together over the past 10 years. There are several ways to measure the softness of the insurance market, including insurance pricing indexes or the available amount of policy holder surplus. The chart tracks capacity in the PRI market since 2001 against Advisen insurance consultants' ADVx Composite Index of general insurance pricing (a pricing benchmark utilized in the insurance industry). The Advisen index shows the change in average pricing in various commercial lines in the United States since 2001.

Figure 3.4 General Insurance Pricing vs. Private PRI Capacity

$ million and index for 2001=100

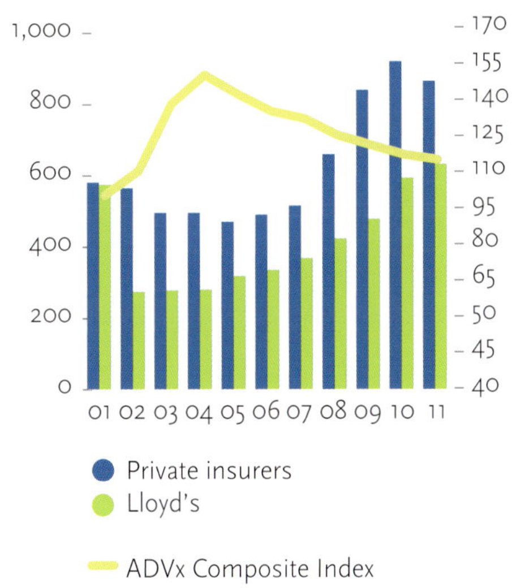

Source: Arthur J. Gallagher & Co., Advisen

General insurance pricing in the United States peaked in 2003, largely as a result of low investment income and insurers' need to replenish capital after the payouts associated with catastrophe losses related to September 11, 2001. At the time, the industry came from a distinctly soft period in the market that had developed during the stock market boom of the 1990s. September 11, 2001 brought the largest catastrophe losses in the industry's history and, coupled with the economic downturn, led to a tightening of market conditions. However, the relationship between loss events and the insurance cycle is not always linear and also depends on the level of accumulated reserves and investment income. For example, in 2005 Hurricane Katrina resulted in catastrophe losses on a scale exceeding those of September 11, 2001, but failed to lead to a new hardening of the market. Buoyant investment yields and liquid financial markets allowed insurers to weather losses.

The insurance cycle is driven by a myriad of factors, but eventually, as in other markets, it is subject to the laws of supply and demand. Insurance supply is determined by insurers' capital position, which in turn depends on liquidity and pricing in the reinsurance market and the investment-yield environment. When investment income is high, insurance companies tend to engage in "cash-flow underwriting" (as opposed to "technical underwriting" where pricing follows actuarial measures of risk), by lowering underwriting standards and cutting premium rates to compete for new policyholders.

The current soft insurance market has persisted throughout the crisis. Despite the temporary rise in claims in the aftermath of the global financial crisis, premium levels have steadily declined and capacity has increased in both the general insurance and PRI market. Benign insurance market conditions held up despite the unfavorable environment in financial markets.

Interest rates and investment yields have remained low, but insurance capacity is still plentiful. In contrast with PRI, the real demand for general insurance has remained sluggish as high-income economies are recovering slowly from the 2008 recession. Industry capitalization, or aggregate "policyholders' surplus" (the difference between insurers' assets and liabilities), continued to grow, fueling competition and downward pressure on premium rates. Leverage ratios—such as annual premiums to surplus or loss reserves to surplus—are at record lows, and serve as rough indications of the amount of risk each dollar of surplus is supporting.[55]

According to the Insurance Information Institute (III), property/casualty policyholders' surplus in the United States increased to $564.7 billion in March 2011, up from $556.9 billion in December 2010. As the III says, "to the extent these leverage ratios provide insight into insurers' capacity utilization and the potential supply of insurance, they help explain why some commercial insurance markets have remained 'soft' for so long."[56]

Another driver of primary insurance pricing is capacity and pricing in the reinsurance market. How much insurance providers in any business segment are willing (and able) to underwrite is largely determined by the availability of reinsurance. While reinsurance capacity contracted slightly during the first quarter of 2011, catastrophe losses, particularly in the Pacific region, failed to translate into higher primary insurance rates.[57] According a report from Aon Benfield brokers, reinsurance market capacity is also strong despite the large losses accruing from the December 2010 Queensland floods in Australia, the February 2011 Christchurch earthquake in New Zealand, and the March 2011 tsunami and earthquake in Japan.

It is unclear how long the current soft state of the global insurance market will persist. If the predictions of continued sluggish growth in the developed countries materialize, interest rates and investment income will likely remain subdued for some time. On the other hand, lower economic activity will also reduce the real demand for insurance services.

Advisen's RIMS Benchmark Survey shows that renewal premium rates in the property insurance market continued to fall in 2011, though the softening trend appeared to be bottoming out by the end of the second quarter.[58] Marsh brokers reported continued pricing reductions, but that the trend had appeared to stabilize as a result of high catastrophe losses and declining investment income. So far, the

Box 3.3 Political Risk Insurance and Its Benefits

PRI captures most, but not all, non-commercial risks. It covers political events, including the direct and indirect actions of host governments that negatively impact investments and for which the investor is not compensated. This report focuses on investment insurance.

In addition to providing compensatory value in the event of claims, PRI can help investors access finance and, in some cases, on better terms, increasing the tenors and size of available loans. Investors are often required to get this insurance in order to obtain financing from banks. For lenders, PRI can provide regulatory relief from country-risk provisioning requirements. When provided by multilateral and large national insurers, PRI can also help deter harmful actions by host governments, help resolve investment disputes, and provide access to best practices in environmental and social standards.

Motivations driving the public and private segments of the market are fundamentally different, which is partly reflected in the cover they are able to provide. National PRI providers have strict mandates from their authorities to serve constituent interests and are also bound by foreign policy considerations. Multilateral providers ensure that their activities are consistent with broad developmental goals. Private providers, are motivated by the need to make profit. As a result, national and multilateral providers are usually able to offer longer tenors and higher capacity than private insurers, but private providers can be more responsive to customer needs for product variations or complementary products.

The following are the political risks commonly insured by the PRI industry. There are differences in the terminology and definitions used by the various insurers, particularly between the public and private insurers.

Expropriation
PRI protects against losses caused by host government actions that may reduce or eliminate ownership or control. It covers outright confiscations, expropriations, and nationalizations, as well as losses resulting from a series of acts that over time have an expropriatory effect.

industry has been able to weather the 2011 catastrophe losses without a noticeable effect on primary insurance premium rates. However, more catastrophe losses could potentially reverse the declining pricing trend and cause markets to harden across insurance business lines, including PRI.

The risk appetite, pricing, and capacity of PRI providers will depend as much on loss events outside the narrow PRI industry as on financial losses from, much less the occurrence of, significant political events. To the extent that large catastrophe losses directly influence reinsurance availability and often require private insurers to deploy capital across business lines, the PRI supply cycle depends disproportionately more on events such as natural disasters than on political events such as the Arab Spring.

Product Innovation and Regulatory Takings

While outright nationalization of foreign investments today is less frequent than in the 1960s and 1970s, a more subtle form of governmental interference, "regulatory takings," has come to the fore of investor concerns since the mid-1990s. Regulatory takings

Currency Inconvertibility and Transfer Restrictions
PRI protects against losses arising from an investor's inability to convert local currency into foreign exchange and to transfer it out of the host country. It also covers excessive delays in acquiring foreign exchange. Typically, this coverage applies to the interruption of interest payments or repatriation of capital or dividends resulting from currency restrictions. It does not cover devaluation risk.

Political Violence (War, Terrorism, and Civil Disturbance)
PRI protects against losses resulting from the damage of tangible assets or business interruption caused by war, insurrection, rebellion, revolution, civil war, vandalism, sabotage, civil disturbance, strikes, riots, and terrorism. Coverage usually applies to politically motivated acts. Certain insurers offer terrorism coverage on a stand-alone basis to supplement property insurance policies, which have largely excluded terrorism as a peril since September 11, 2001. Terrorism insurance increasingly offers cover against broader political violence risks.

Breach of Contract/Arbitration Award Default
PRI protects against losses arising from a host government's breach or repudiation of a contractual agreement with an investor. Claims are usually payable only after an investor has invoked a dispute resolution mechanism (such as arbitration), has obtained an award for damages, and the host government has failed to honor the award.

Non-honoring of Sovereign Financial Obligations
PRI protects against losses resulting from a government's failure to make a payment when due under an unconditional financial payment obligation or guarantee given in favor of a project that otherwise meets an insurer's requirements. It does not require the investor to obtain an arbitral award. This coverage is usually applicable in situations when a sovereign's financial payment obligation is unconditional and not subject to defenses.

Source: MIGA and market consultations.

largely comprise unlawful and often discriminatory sets of new regulations that in effect deprive the investor of ownership rights, or impair the value of an investment to an extent that it is deemed to be expropriated.

Regulatory expropriation, including "creeping" or "indirect" expropriation, can come in many shapes and forms and includes renegotiation of concessions, changes in the terms of commercial agreements, discriminatory fees or taxes, or the failure of governments to enforce property rights. The challenge is to distinguish between legitimate and unlawful actions. Renegotiations of large infrastructure contracts, for example, are the rule rather than the exception. In a data set of one thousand infrastructure projects awarded in Latin America between 1985 and 2000, a 2004 World Bank study estimated that 30 percent of all contracts were renegotiated.[59]

Periods of social and economic change will almost inevitably lead to shifts in public policy. These shifts in policy may embrace a wide range of views, including a more statist stewardship of national economies, a change in the level of enforcement of property rights, greater reliance on state-owned enterprises, or large discoveries of natural resources. In all these circumstances it is reasonable to expect changes in the regulatory framework and its enforcement. Even if involving a financially negative effect on investors, such regulatory changes may not always be unlawful. After all, the ability to regulate sectors of the domestic economy is an inherent attribute of state sovereignty.

To identify regulatory takings, and distinguish between legitimate and unlawful regulatory intervention, both procedural and substantive characteristics of the government intervention need examination. These include, among other issues: (a) whether the regulation interfered with recognized property rights of the investor, (b) whether the regulation was enacted for a public purpose, was non-discriminatory, followed due process, and was proportional, and (c) whether the economic impact is substantial enough to warrant compensation. However, there is still no single and internationally recognized definition of regulatory takings that enables expropriatory and legitimate regulation to be distinguished on a consistent basis.

The PRI industry has tried to keep pace with the changing nature of political perils, including adverse effects of regulatory changes, and adapt its products to the changing needs of the marketplace. But the absence of an internationally accepted legal definition of regulatory takings has meant that the PRI industry has not been able to offer a standardized insurance product that addresses this particular risk. Instead of developing a stand-alone product for regulatory risk, some insurers have decided to broaden the scope of their conventional expropriation cover.

Traditionally, expropriations have been defined in PRI policies as actions of governments that cause a full cessation of operations, deprive property, or prevent the control of funds. PRI policies typically exclude bona fide acts of governments that are non-discriminatory and taken in the public interest. To extend the scope of expropriation coverage some insurers have deliberately opened the above criteria to a broader set of contingencies. MIGA's contract of guarantee, for instance, defines actions of expropriation as "any direct or indirect action or inaction, in one or a series of events", thus including omissions by governments. "Series of events" was added to protect investors against "creeping expropriation," in which the cumulative effect of a number of government interventions result in the loss of a substantial portion of the guaranteed investment.[60]

However, there are inherent limits to which the traditional expropriation coverage can be extended to cover regulatory risk. In standard expropriation coverage, a claim payment gives the insurer a right of subrogation on the indemnified assets and allows the insurer to seek recovery from the expropriating government at a later stage. In the case of regulatory takings, subrogation and recovery are hard to come by as the investor often has not been deprived of ownership rights, and the extraction of economic value is often the motivation for regulatory intervention in the first place. As recovery prospects are built into insurers' pricing models, a broader application of the expropriation product would require insurers to restructure and reprice insurance policies accordingly. Moreover, the difficulty of defining regulatory takings further complicates the estimation of claim frequencies for insurers, and would likely significantly restrict the duration of contract tenors.

Corporate Approaches to Political Risk Management

On the PRI demand side, as more firms invest in

more countries around the world, their ability to assess and manage political risk becomes more important, and political risk analysis becomes an integral component of the investment location process. With political risks increasing, more multinational investors are putting in place political risk management processes. Such processes are quite diverse, ranging from monitoring political developments to applying contractual risk-mitigation tools such as PRI. As awareness of potentially significant losses arising from political events has grown over time, more companies are asking corporate risk officers to manage these risks. As described above, real demand for PRI is driven by a combination of increasing FDI flows, greater risk aversion including awareness of political risk, and increasing sophistication of risk-management processes.

PRI is by no means the most widespread form of political risk mitigation. Most of the firms responding to the MIGA-EIU surveys address political risks through concluding joint ventures with domestic partners, exercising caution by implementing investment plans gradually, and performing political risk analysis and monitoring developments (figure 3.5). Only one in five firms surveyed in 2011 used investment insurance to mitigate political risk, a proportion that has not changed from last year. The use of PRI also varies by sector. Of the firms MIGA surveyed in the primary and utilities sectors, 28 percent and 27 percent respectively reported using PRI as a tool to mitigate political risk. In the financial services sector, 25 percent of the firms surveyed reported using PRI, followed by manufacturing (21 percent) and non-financial services (12 percent).

The perceived usefulness of risk-mitigation tools also varies significantly by type of political risk (figure 3.6). For example, informal risk mitigation through engagement with key political figures or local communities remains the most prevalent approach used by foreign investors to mitigate expropriation. In the case of political violence, many investors seem to believe that no risk-mitigation tool can effectively alleviate this risk, despite the fact that PRI is a viable and available option. PRI was not perceived to be an effective tool for mitigating regulatory risk, which investors cited as the risk of most concern in this year's survey—and the one that is rarely eligible for investment guarantee coverage.

Figure 3.5 Tools Used to Mitigate Political Risk in Developing Countries

Percent of respondents

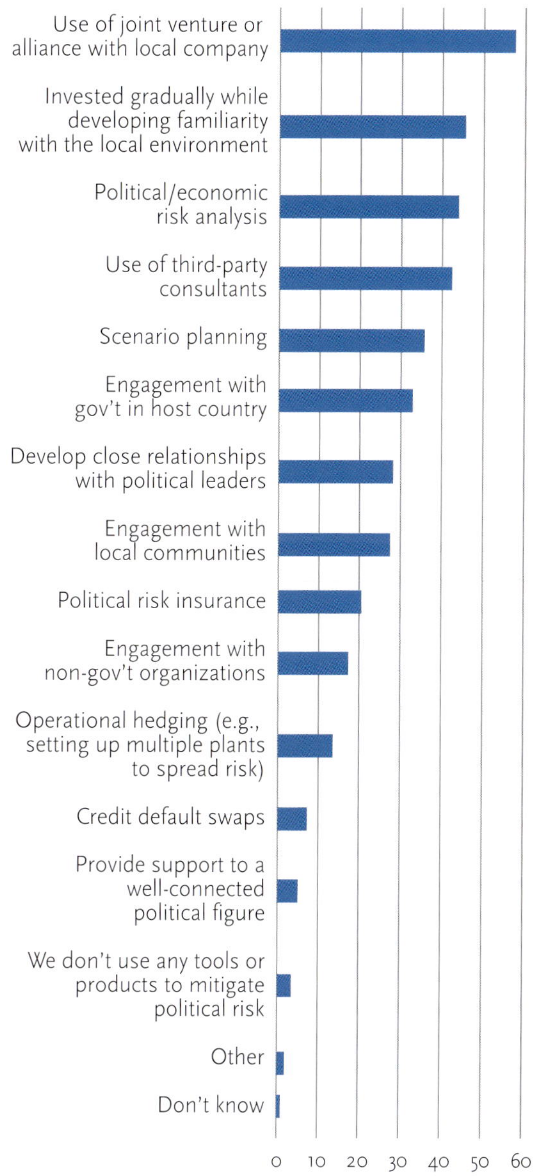

Source: MIGA-EIU Political Risk Survey 2011.

Figure 3.6 Most Effective Tools Used to Mitigate Political Risk in Developing Countries by Type of Risk

Percent of respondents

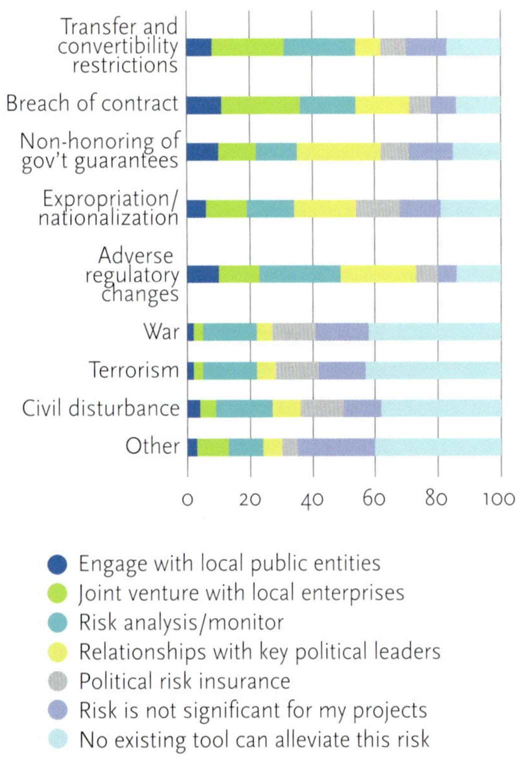

Source: MIGA-EIU Political Risk Survey 2011.

Despite the longer-term trend of an increasing real demand for PRI, a majority of risk managers are still either agnostic as to how political risk can be mitigated most effectively, or prefer informal mitigation methods—that is, risk assessments and relationships with key political leaders. Most likely, this is because the value of political risk protection is inherently difficult to monetize. As political risk is hard to quantify in terms of probability and severity ex-ante, cost-benefit calculations to determine the value of PRI are difficult. But the reliance on informal risk-mitigation tools also begs the question of the extent to which firms might be exhibiting a degree of overconfidence in addressing political risk, for relationships with key political leaders are an effective risk-mitigation tool only so long as those leaders are in power. PRI, on the other hand, can be a very effective tool to hedge against cataclysmic and unexpected risk events such as the Arab Spring.

This is not to say that contractual risk mitigation through PRI should be the only instrument used by MNEs to manage political risk. Instead PRI should be regarded by MNEs as a supplement to a broader strategy of engagement with the host country society, including contacts with civil society groups or local business alliances. Furthermore, in periods of profound uncertainty and rapid change, PRI can give comfort to investors who simply lack sufficient confidence in an institutional environment, even when economic fundamentals appear to be sound.

The perception of expropriation risk discussed in Chapter Two is a case in point. As the chapter shows, there is a sizeable disconnect between risk perceptions of investors and PRI underwriters over the likelihood of expropriation in different types of political regimes. In preparation for this report, MIGA conducted discussions with the private market about underwriting practices in different regime type environments. Broadly speaking, most PRI insurers agree that there is a higher propensity for non-democratic regimes to follow through with expropriations, and that lower recovery prospects are directly priced in risk assessment methods.

Since a pay-out on a PRI contract arises from a governmental action that changed pre-existing rights (for example, over ownership, management, or control of assets), most recoveries are focused on claiming a breach of existing of rights and asking the government for compensation. In the experience of PRI providers, this process is most likely to be successful in countries with judicial redress and where multiple actors can be appealed to in order to right the wrong. Such regimes tend to be democratic.

Like investors, the private market is also concerned about the risk of policy discontinuity arising from governmental changes—even in democratic regimes. In addition, the most significant risk for insurers relates to the existing exposure and, in case of a turn for the worse in the policy environment, the key risk factors that private political risk insurers look to are related to ease of recovery.

The MENA Region and the Arab Spring

Aside from the geopolitical hotspots of Iran, Iraq, and the West Bank and Gaza, the MENA region has not traditionally been perceived by foreign investors as particularly prone to political risk. In fact, overall, many investors had perceived the region as largely stable and predictable. This view is borne out by BU data on regional PRI issuance. New PRI business issued in MENA since 2005, scaled by FDI flows, has been broadly in line with emerging-market averages. In the years between 2007 and 2009, the trend for new PRI issuance in the region was markedly lower than in the rest of developing economies, though PRI issuance rebounded in 2010 (see figure 3.7). PRI contracts in MENA as a share of BU members' global liability portfolios were stable at around 8 percent.

Most MENA countries were stable for a very long time indeed. On average, political leaders of the region have been in power for more than 17 years. The former presidents of Egypt, Libya, and, Tunisia held office for 30, 42, and 24 years, respectively. However, political stability—defined backward-looking as the longevity of a particular regime—is seldom a good predictor of prevailing structural political risk.

Various editions of the Arab Human Development Report, prepared by the United Nations Development Program since 2002, argued that the region's demographic structure, labor markets, civic life, private enterprise, and income distribution had made it a much less stable region than was widely believed. "The Middle East region is more complex, more fragile, and more dangerous than it has been for a very long time. [...] There are a number of growing causes of instability and uncertainty in this region," the authors wrote in 2009.[61]

Compared with other regions, Arab societies are overwhelmingly young and urbanized. By 2005, 60 percent of Arabs were estimated to be younger than 25, with a median age of 22. The global average age is 28. Fifty-five percent of the Arab population was estimated to live in cities. In addition, real economic growth across the Arab world has been slow, often lagging behind population growth. Real per capita gross domestic product growth since 1980 was less than 0.5 percent annually. As a result, unemployment rates among Arab youth have been persistently high for many years, exceeding corresponding unemployment rates in Latin America or Asia by sometimes well over 10 percent.

Further, unemployment in MENA tends to fall disproportionately on the young. Youth unemployment is twice as high as the global average, and labor force participation is especially low among Arab women.[62] The World Bank warned in a 2009 report on private sector development in the Arab World that an estimated 40 million jobs had to be created in the private sector over the coming decade to provide opportunities for a growing, young, and increasingly educated labor force.[63]

Figure 3.7 Ratio of New PRI to FDI for Developing Countries and MENA; PRI Exposure in Developing Countries and MENA

$ billion and percent

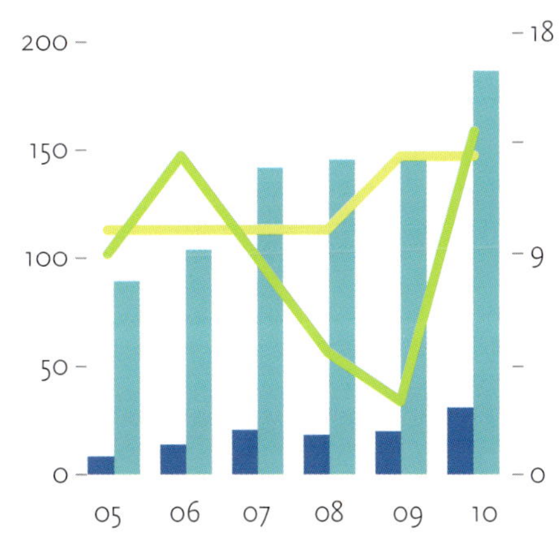

Source: Berne Union, World Bank.

Anemic job creation and economic growth are a direct corollary to an underperforming private sector. Particularly in developing (non-oil exporting) MENA economies, the private sector's contribution to domestic capital formation—a measure of investments by businesses—is low by comparison: in some countries this contribution is more than 50 percent less than the world average, and correlates with lower real growth rates. Insufficient reliance on private enterprise and businesses has precluded some MENA economies from undergoing an effective process of economic diversification, including a greater reliance on outward-oriented sectors. Consequently, MENA economies score low in measures such as export diversification or contribution of exports to real economic growth. Indeed, by some accounts MENA economies have de-industrialized since the 1970s, taking into consideration manufacturing as a share of GDP.[64]

Much of this private sector underperformance is due to the discretionary implementation of regulatory policies and a lack of government credibility, as several reports have pointed out. Firm-level survey findings conducted by the World Bank show that issues related to the rule of law, property rights, and favoritism are among the top concerns of local business communities in many MENA countries.[65] At a micro-level, such as in firm and household-level survey data, political risk in the MENA region was very much apparent.

Furthermore, stagnating income levels, latent food insecurity, unemployment, and the lack of social perspectives have exacerbated a sense of political disenfranchisement and mistrust toward the public sector. Egypt experienced its first severe bread unrest under former ruler Anwar al-Sadat in 1977. Bread riots tipped Tunisia into turmoil as early as 1984. Consequently, when bread prices soared in early 2008, Egyptian newspaper columnists began to proclaim that the country was headed for a "revolution of the hungry."

In conclusion, a long period of political stability in the MENA region masked social tensions and the heightened risk of an outbreak of public discontent. Relatively low levels of domestic private investment should have been a sign of a difficult business environment, and combined with mounting demographic and economic pressures, an indication of growing political risk. Clearly, predicting the timing and outbreak of social upheavals such as the Arab Spring will always be elusive. However, the difficulty of predicting the occurrence of such political events does not preclude risk analysts from paying careful attention to underlying economic, social, and demographic factors that can point to an elevated level of structural political risk. PRI, whose financial value is difficult to quantify on the basis of probabilistic metrics, remains an effective hedge to protect investments in times of political change and stress.

ENDNOTES

Endnotes

[1] Data on M&As and greenfield investments are from the United Nations Conference on Trade and Development (UNCTAD), World Investment Report 2011.

[2] MIGA. 2010. World Investment and Political Risk 2010. Washington DC: World Bank.

[3] China's State Administration of Foreign Exchange has recently revised FDI flows into China (and other items in the financial account) to better capture reinvested earnings of foreign affiliates.

[4] UNCTAD. World Investment Report 2011. Geneva: UNCTAD.

[5] Based on the World Bank's Harmonized List of Fragile Situations FY12, which consists of IDA-eligible countries with a harmonized CPIA country rating of 3.2 or less and countries with a UN and/or regional peace-keeping or peace building mission during the past three years.

[6] Ernst & Young. 2011 Africa Attractiveness Survey: It's Time for Africa.

[7] Ernst & Young. 2011 India Attractiveness Survey: Reaching Towards its True Potential.

[8] For a discussion of FDI from developing countries see Global Development Horizons 2011 (Washington, DC, World Bank).

[9] Institute of World Economy and International Relations of the Russian Academy of Sciences and VCC. June 23, 2011. Investment from Russia Stabilizes after the Global Crisis.

[10] Grant Thornton. Mergers and Acquisitions: Global Prospects for Growth 2011. Six thousand privately held companies across 39 economies were surveyed.

[11] Aon. Political Risk Map 2011.

[12] Maplecroft. Political Risk Atlas 2011.

[13] Belize Electricity Ltd., majority-owned by Fortis Inc. (Canada). Case in courts.

[14] First Quantum Minerals (Canada).

[15] "Venezuelan Government Has Seized 988 Companies." El Universal. August 29, 2011.

[16] The Fraser Institute. Survey of Mining Companies 2010/2011. Vancouver, Canada: The Fraser Institute.

[17] Maplecroft. The Sub-National Map of the Water Stress Index 2011. (online at http://www.ipoliticalrisk.com/2011/05/maplecroft-examines-water-stressed.html).

[18] UNCTAD, op. cit.

[19] Ernst & Young in collaboration with Oxford Analytica. Turn Risks and Opportunities into Results. 2011.

[20] "Effects of Japan Disaster on Global Supply Chain Still Unknown." Minyanville. March 29, 2011.

[21] Bill McBeath. 2011. Urgency for Supply Chain Resilience: Results from ChainLink's 2011 Supply Chain Risk Survey.

[22] Such as OECD Principles of Corporate Governance, OECD Convention on Combating Bribery of Foreign Public Officials in International Business Transactions, United Nations Convention Against Corruption.

[23] For more information on EITI, see http://eiti.org/.

[24] Economist Intelligence Unit and VCC. 2007. World Investment Prospects to 2011: Foreign Direct Investment and the Challenge of Political Risk. New York: VCC and EIU.

[25] This finding was also documented in MIGA's World Investment and Political Risk 2009 (Washington DC, World Bank).

[26] UNCTAD-OECD. 2011. The UNCTAD-OECD Report on G20 Investment Measures.

[27] Unless otherwise specified, the MENA region excludes high-income countries.

[28] Central Bank of Egypt. August 25, 2011. Press Release.

[29] Global Arab Network. September 15, 2011. "Tunisia: Industry Looking to Rebound."

[30] World Bank. 2011, Investing for Growth and Jobs. World Bank: Washington, DC.

[31] Central Bank of Egypt, August 2011, Monthly Statistical Bulletin and Central Bank of Tunisia, Development of Main Flows and Balance of External Payments Receipts (online: http://www.bct.gov.tn/bct/siteprod/english/indicateurs/paiements.jsp#qqind).

[32] UNCTAD, op. cit.

[33] Freund, C. and L. Mottaghi. 2011. Transition to Democracy. World Bank: Washington, DC.

[34] Farzaneh Roudi. 2011. Youth Population and Employment in the Middle East and North Africa: Opportunity or Challenge? United Nations Department of Economic and Social Affairs: New York.

[35] The European Union has singed Association Agreements with these countries.

[36] "Qatar pledges $10 billion investment in Egypt." AFP. May 28, 2011.

[37] Grant Thornton's International Business Report 2011 surveyed 2,697 medium to large privately owned companies worldwide. For more information, see http://www.internationalbusinessreport.com/.

[38] Business Law Currents. August 25, 2011. "Arab Spring Cleaning: What Regional Turmoil Has Meant for Western Investment."

[39] For research that looks at the propensity to expropriate on the basis of regimes types, see Quan Li, 2009, "Democracy, Autocracy, and Expropriation of Foreign Direct Investment," Comparative Political Studies. This work looks at pre-conditions that activate the propensity to expropriate.

[40] Michael Tomz and Mark Wright. 2010. "Sovereign Theft: Theory and Evidence about Default and Expropriation." In The Natural Resource Trap: Private Investment without Public Commitment, ed. William Hogan and Federico Sturzenegger. Cambridge, MA: MIT Press. Also Nathan Jensen and Noel P. Johnston. 2010. "Political Risk, Reputation, and the Resource Curse." St. Louis, MO: Washington University.

[41] Data by S. Kobrin cited in "Expropriation of Foreign Direct Investments: Sectoral Patterns from 1993 to 2006," Chris Hajzler, University of Otago, Economics Discussion Paper No. 1011.

[42] Michael Minor. 1994. "The Demise of Expropriation as an Instrument of LDC Policy: 1980-1992.",Journal of International Business Studies.

[43] Chris Hajzler. "Expropriation of Foreign Direct Investments: Sectoral Patterns from 1993 to 2006." Otago, New Zealand: University of Otago.

[44] M. Minor, op. cit.

[45] Chris Hajzler, op. cit.

[46] Ibid.

[47] This section summarizes the initial findings of a joint research effort by Nathan Jensen (Washington University, St. Louis) and Daniel Villar (MIGA). Detailed findings are being prepared for an academic journal.

[48] MIGA is not making an attempt to opine on the validity of the underlying data of expropriations and disputes. The existence of what PRI providers have accepted as expropriation claims and what a respected arbitration forum has accepted as a dispute is used as a data point to determine correlations among variables.

[49] Quan Li. 2009. "Democracy, Autocracy, and Expropriation of Foreign Direct Investment." Comparative Political Studies.

[50] UNCTAD, op. cit.

[51] Marsh 2011 Insurance Market Midyear Update

[52] African Trade Insurance Agency. March 11, 2011. "Turmoil in the MENA region & Increased Risk Premiums Prompts Insurers to Strengthen Support to Exporters and Investors." Press release

[53] "Rich Rush for Insurance Cover Amid Middle East Turmoil." The Guardian. March 5, 2011.

[54] Capacity here refers to total possible maximum USD (in millions) per risk.

[55] Verisk Analytics. June 22, 2011. "Property/Casualty Insurers' Profits And Profitability Fell In First Quarter 2011 As Net Losses On Underwriting Ballooned." Press Release.

[56] Ibid.

[57] Aon Reinsurance Market Outlook. June/July 2011.

[58] Rims. August 11, 2011. "Soft Market May be Near Bottom, According to Latest RIMS Benchmark Survey." Press Release.

[59] Guasch, J.L. 2004. Granting and Renegotiating Infrastructure Projects: Doing it Right. Washington, DC: World Bank Institute.

[60] As per MIGA's contract of guarantee, a loss can also include "[depriving] the guarantee holder or the project enterprise of a substantial benefit of the guaranteed investment constituting a fundamental right essential to the overall financial viability of the guaranteed investment and/or the project enterprise."

[61] UNDP. 2009. Arab Human Development Report 2009. UNDP: New York.

[62] Demographic and economic data cited are all World Bank statistics (World Development Indicators, 2011).

[63] World Bank. 2009. From Privilege to Competition – Unlocking Private-led Growth in the Middle East and North Africa. World Bank: Washington, DC.

[64] UNDP. 2009. Arab Human Development Report 2009. UNDP: New York.

[65] Ibid.

APPENDICES

Appendix 1 FDI Inflows, 2003–2010

$ billion

	2003	2004	2005	2006	2007	2008	2009	2010[e]
World	646	784	1183	1576	2341	1918	950	881
Developed countries	493	576	871	1,185	1,810	1,303	869	800
Developing countries	153	207	312	391	531	614	81	81
Latin America and the Carribbean	43.3	65.9	72.2	72.0	109.4	127.9	73.6	112.6
Argentina	1.65	4.12	5.27	5.54	6.47	9.73	4.01	6.34
Brazil	10.14	18.17	15.07	18.78	34.58	45.06	25.95	48.44
Chile	4.31	7.17	6.98	7.30	12.53	15.18	12.70	15.10
Colombia	1.72	3.02	10.25	6.66	9.05	10.60	7.26	6.77
Costa Rica	0.58	0.79	0.86	1.47	1.90	2.08	1.35	1.47
Dominican Republic	0.61	0.91	1.12	1.08	1.67	2.87	2.07	1.63
Jamaica	0.72	0.60	0.68	0.88	0.87	1.44	0.54	0.23
Mexico	16.59	23.82	22.34	19.78	27.31	23.17	11.42	18.68
Peru	1.34	1.60	2.58	3.47	5.49	6.92	4.76	7.33
Uruguay	0.42	0.33	0.85	1.49	1.32	2.21	1.14	1.63
Venezuela, R.B. de	2.04	1.48	2.60	(0.51)	1.01	0.35	(3.11)	(1.40)
East Asia and the Pacific	57.1	71.0	143.1	153.1	200.7	215.1	138.4	227.6
China	47.08	54.94	117.21	24.08	60.05	175.15	114.22	185.08
Indonesia	(0.60)	1.90	8.34	4.91	6.93	9.32	4.88	13.30
Malaysia	2.47	4.62	3.97	6.08	8.45	7.38	1.61	9.51
Philippines	0.49	0.69	1.85	2.92	2.92	1.54	1.95	1.71
Thailand	5.23	5.86	8.06	9.45	11.32	8.57	5.96	6.31
Vietnam	1.45	1.61	1.95	2.40	6.70	9.58	7.60	8.00
South Asia	5.4	7.6	11.2	26.0	32.3	48.7	38.3	28.0
Bangladesh	0.27	0.45	0.81	0.70	0.65	1.01	0.67	0.97
India	4.32	5.77	7.61	20.34	25.13	41.17	34.58	24.16
Pakistan	0.53	1.12	2.20	4.27	5.59	5.44	2.39	2.02
Sri Lanka	0.23	0.23	0.27	0.48	0.60	0.75	0.40	0.48
Europe and Central Asia	23.8	41.9	51.1	92.5	132.6	158.9	86.0	84.9
Belarus	0.17	0.16	0.31	0.35	1.79	2.18	1.88	1.35
Bosnia and Herzegovina	0.38	0.71	0.61	0.77	2.07	0.92	0.23	0.07
Bulgaria	2.10	2.66	4.31	7.76	13.21	9.94	4.49	2.17
Kazakhstan	2.09	4.16	1.97	6.28	11.12	15.78	12.60	9.96
Romania	1.84	6.44	6.48	11.39	9.93	13.88	6.31	3.45
Russian Federation	7.96	15.44	12.89	29.70	55.07	75.00	37.13	42.87
Turkey	1.70	2.79	10.03	20.19	22.05	18.27	7.96	9.28
Ukraine	1.42	1.72	7.81	5.60	9.89	10.91	4.82	6.50

Appendix 1 FDI Inflows, 2003–2010 (cont'd)

$ billion

	2003	2004	2005	2006	2007	2008	2009	2010^e
Middle East and North Africa	10.0	9.7	16.8	27.2	27.6	29.3	24.4	22.7
Algeria	0.63	0.88	1.08	1.80	1.66	2.65	2.85	2.29
Egypt, Arab Rep.	0.24	1.25	5.38	10.04	11.58	9.49	6.71	6.39
Iran, Islamic Rep.	2.70	2.86	3.14	1.65	1.67	1.62	3.02	3.62
Jordan	0.55	0.94	1.98	3.54	2.62	2.83	2.38	1.70
Lebanon	2.86	1.90	2.62	2.67	3.38	4.33	4.80	4.95
Morocco	2.31	0.79	1.62	2.37	2.81	2.47	1.33	1.24
Syrian Arab Republic	0.16	0.28	0.50	0.66	1.24	1.47	1.43	1.38
Tunisia	0.59	0.64	0.72	3.27	1.53	2.64	1.60	1.40
Sub-Saharan Africa	13.3	11.0	18.0	20.2	28.5	34.5	30.4	31.1
Angola	3.50	1.45	(1.30)	(0.04)	(0.89)	1.68	2.21	2.05
Botswana	0.42	0.39	0.28	0.49	0.65	0.11	0.23	0.53
Congo, Dem. Rep.	0.39	0.41	..	0.26	1.81	1.73	0.95	2.96
Congo, Rep.	0.32	(0.01)	0.51	1.49	2.64	2.48	2.08	2.82
Ghana	0.14	0.14	0.14	0.64	0.97	2.11	1.68	2.53
Liberia	0.37	0.08	0.08	0.11	0.13	0.14	0.38	0.45
Madagascar	0.01	0.05	0.09	0.29	0.78	1.11	1.38	0.86
Mauritius	0.06	0.01	0.04	0.11	0.34	0.38	0.26	0.43
Mozambique	0.34	0.24	0.11	0.15	0.43	0.59	0.88	0.79
Niger	0.01	0.03	0.04	0.05	0.13	0.57	0.74	0.74
Nigeria	2.01	1.87	4.98	8.82	6.03	4.88	5.79	6.05
Seychelles	0.06	0.04	0.09	0.15	0.25	0.24	0.25	0.37
South Africa	0.78	0.70	6.52	(0.18)	5.74	9.64	5.63	1.57
Sudan	1.35	1.51	2.30	3.53	2.43	2.60	2.92	2.89
Swaziland	(0.06)	0.07	(0.05)	0.12	0.04	0.11	0.07	0.09
Uganda	0.20	0.30	0.38	0.64	0.79	0.73	0.60	0.82
Zambia	0.35	0.36	0.36	0.62	1.32	0.94	0.70	1.04

Source: World Bank.
Note: Figures in parentheses represent negative numbers; e=estimate.

Appendix 2 MIGA-EIU Political Risk Survey 2011

The data provided herein are based on a survey conducted on behalf of MIGA by the Economist Intelligence Unit. The survey, which was carried out in June/July 2011, contains the responses of 316 senior executives from multinational enterprises investing in developing countries. Eighteen percent of the respondents in the 2011 survey also participated in the MIGA-EIU Political Risk Surveys of 2009 and 2010. Quota sampling was used to ensure that the industry and geographic composition of the survey sample approximates the composition of actual FDI outflows to developing countries: following a first round of responses to the questionnaire, additional email campaigns targeting respondents in specific industries or geographic locations were conducted until all demographic quotas were met. For some questions, percentages add up to more than 100 percent because of multiple selections.

Figure A2.1 What is your industry sector?

Percent of respondents

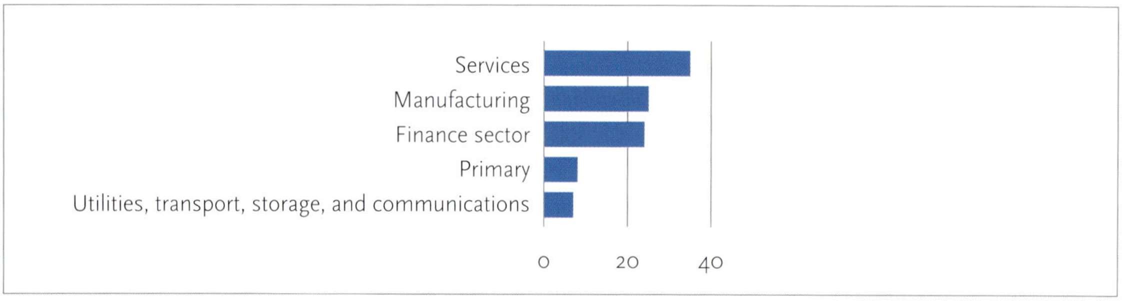

Figure A2.2 What are your organization's global annual revenues?

Percent of respondents

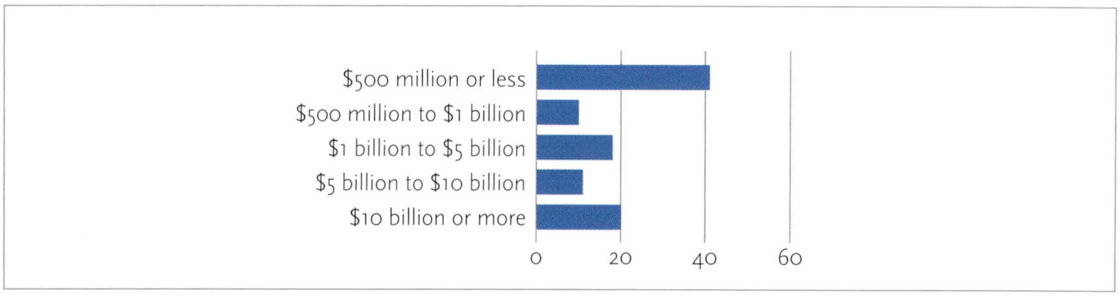

Figure A2.3 In which region is your company headquarters located?

Number of respondents

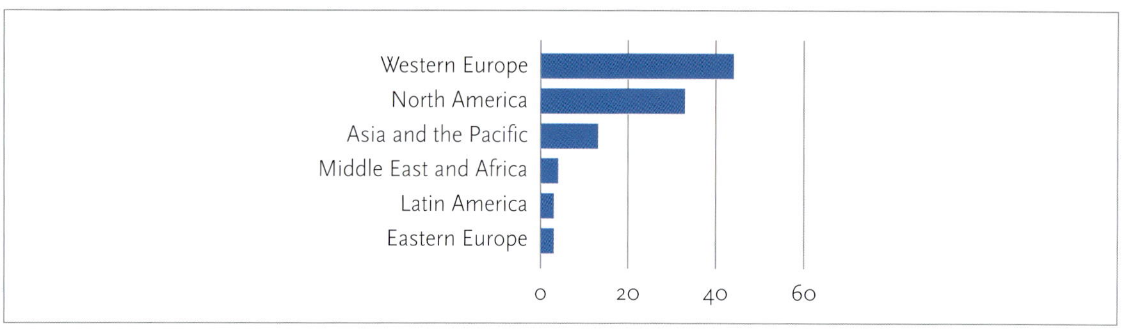

Question 1. In which developing countries is your firm presently investing?

Percent of respondents

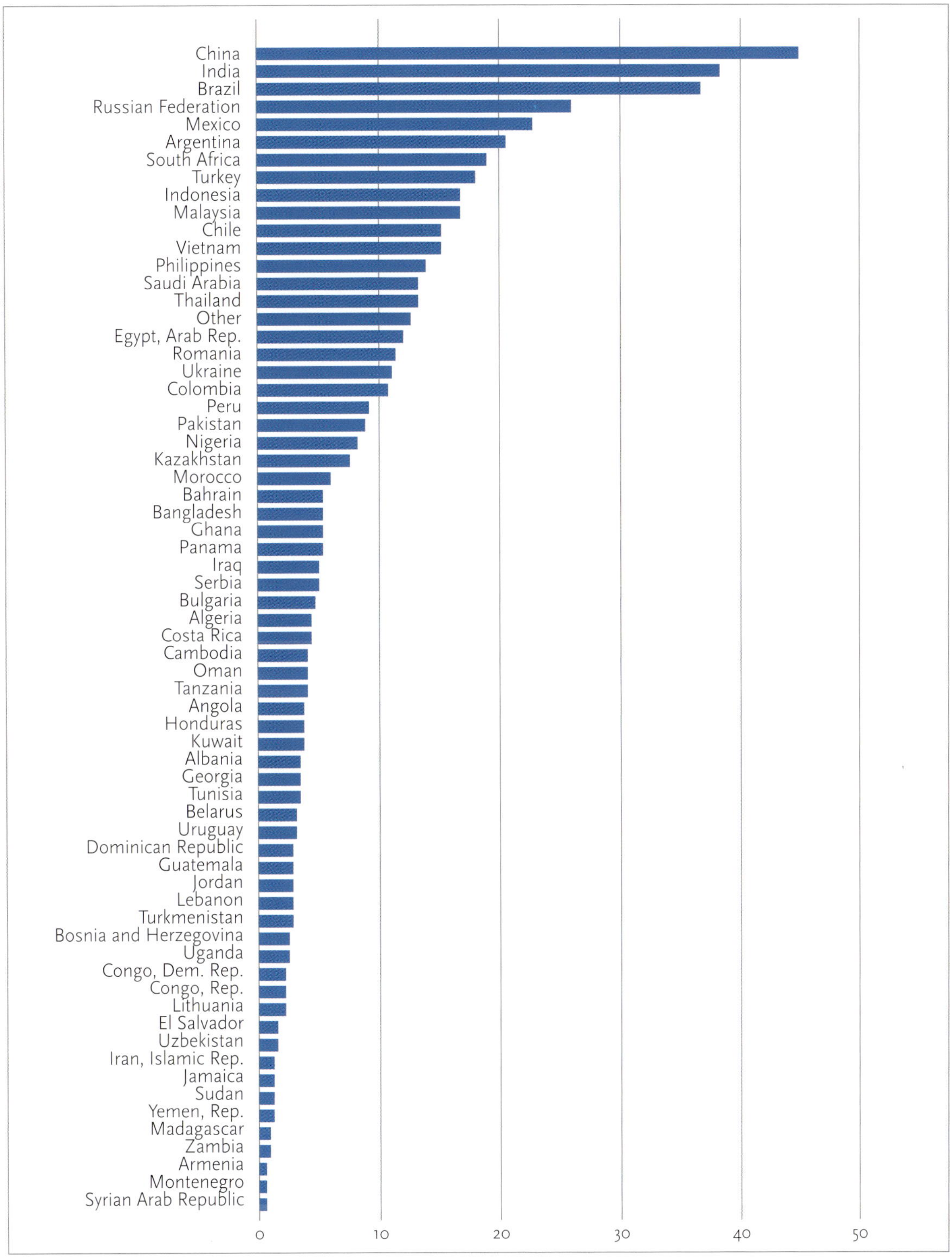

Question 2. How do you expect your company's planned investments in emerging markets to change this year compared with last year and over the next three years compared with the previous three years?

Percent of respondents

This year compared with last year
Percent of respondents

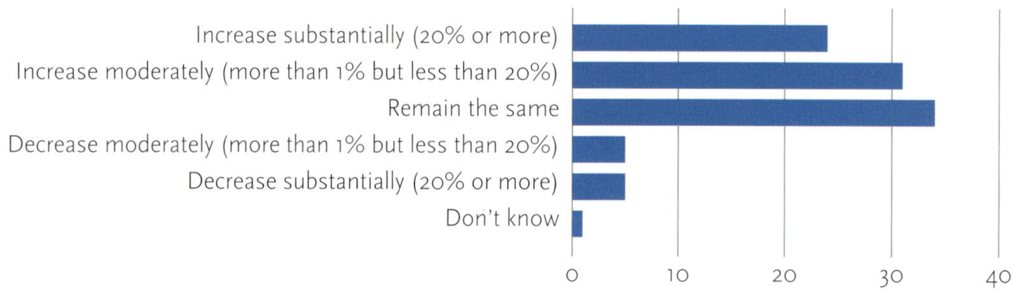

Over the next three years compared with the previous three years
Percent of respondents

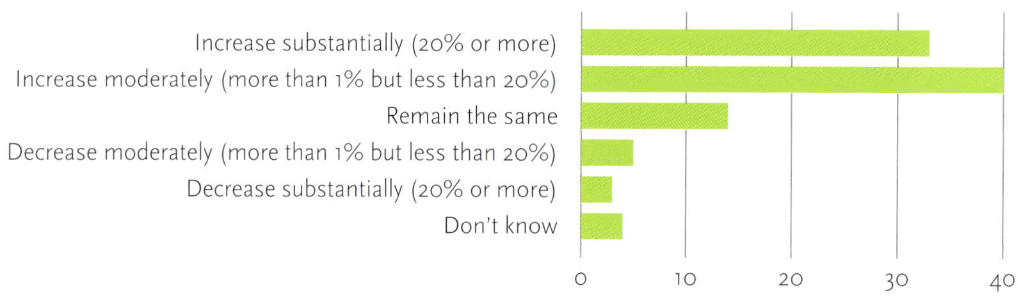

Question 3. What is the greatest constraint to cross-border investments in developing countries in the next 12 months and in the next three years?

Percent of respondents

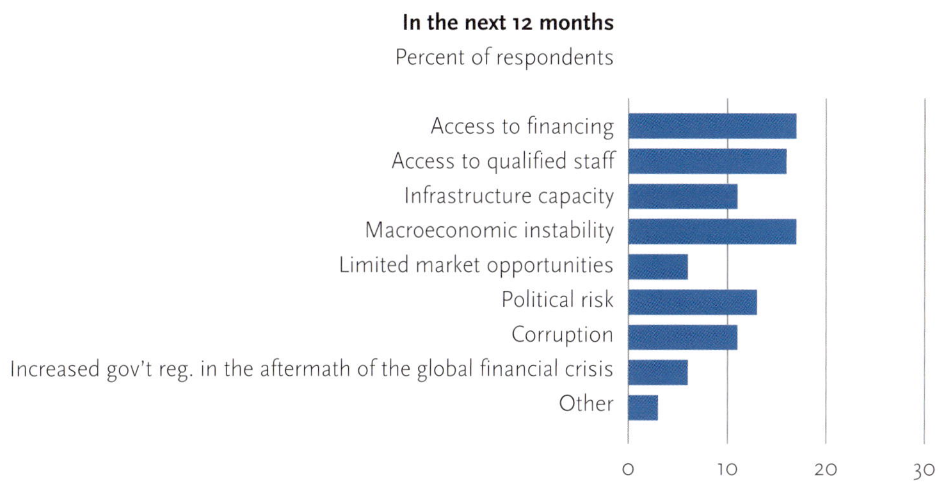

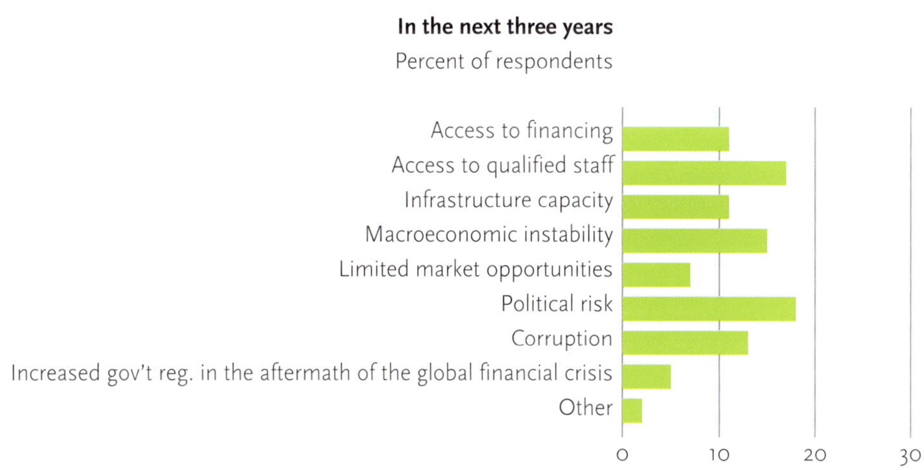

Question 3a. What is the greatest constraint to cross-border investments in developing countries in the next 12 months and in the next three years?

Percent of respondents

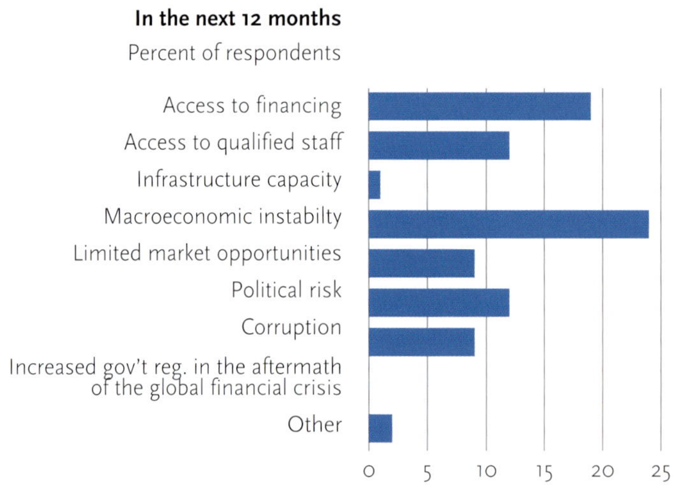

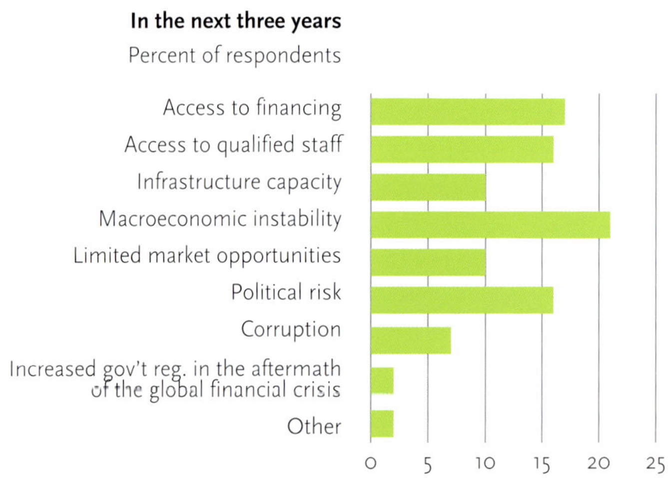

Note: *These findings apply to 18 percent of respondents in the MIGA-EIU political risk survey 2011 who also participated in the MIGA-EIU Political Risk Surveys for 2009 and 2010.*

Question 3b. What is the greatest constraint to cross-border investments in developing countries in the next 12 months and in the next three years? (Responses of South investors)

Percent of respondents

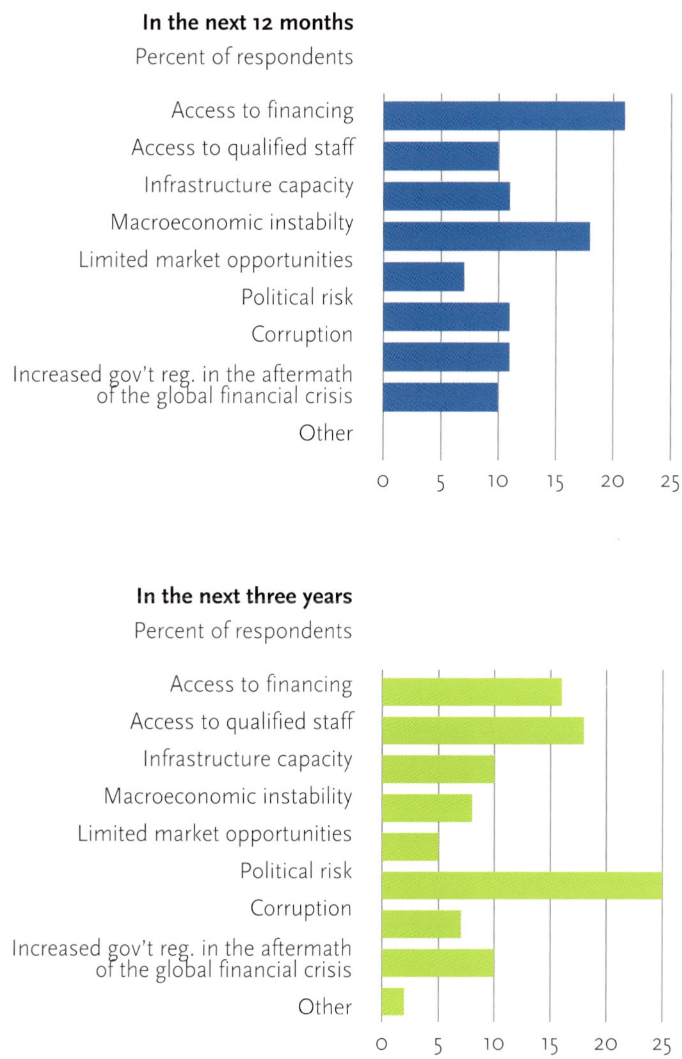

Question 4. Which types of political risk are of most concern to your company when investing in developing countries?

Percent of respondents

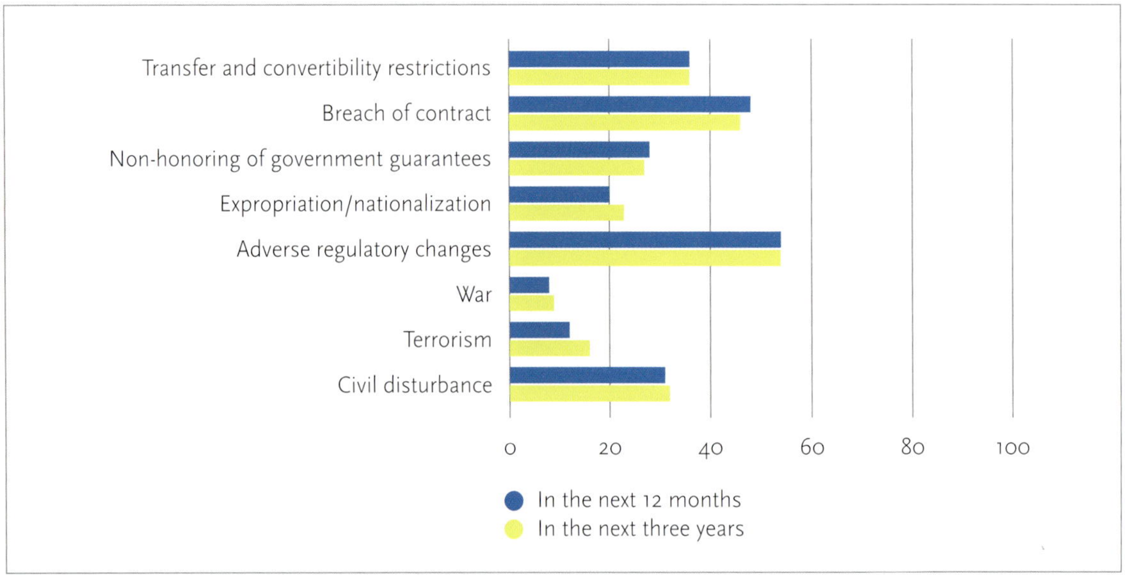

Question 5. In the developing countries where your company invests presently, how do each of the risks listed below affect your company?

Percent of respondents

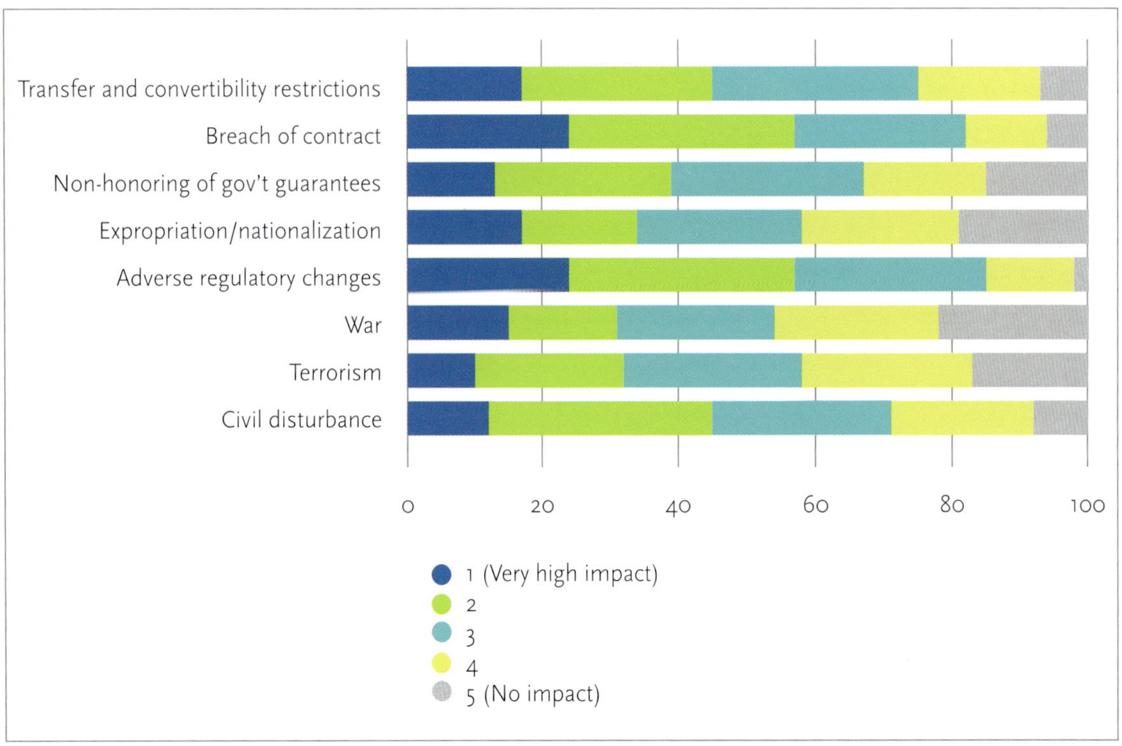

Question 6. In the past three years has your company experienced financial losses caused by any of the following risks?

Percent of respondents

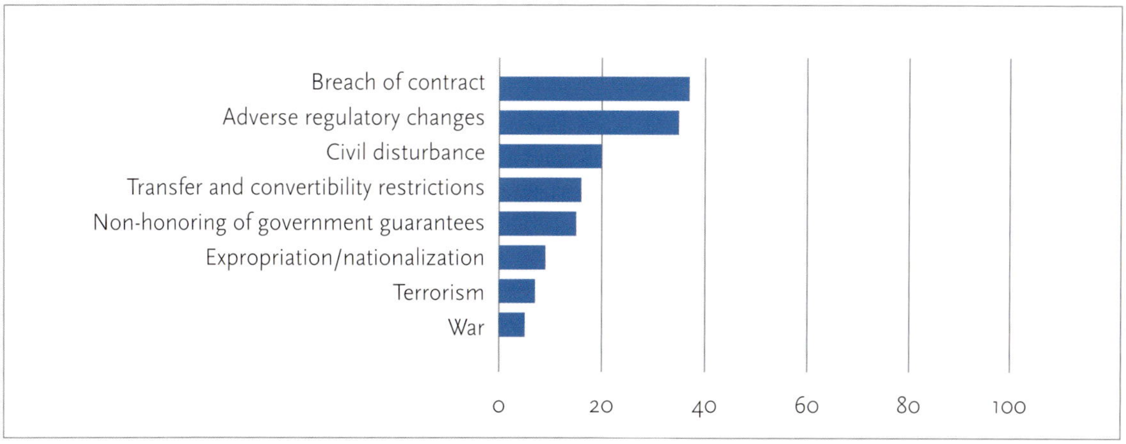

Question 7. To your knowledge, have any of the following risks caused your company to withdraw an existing investment or cancel planned investments over the past 12 months?

Percent of respondents

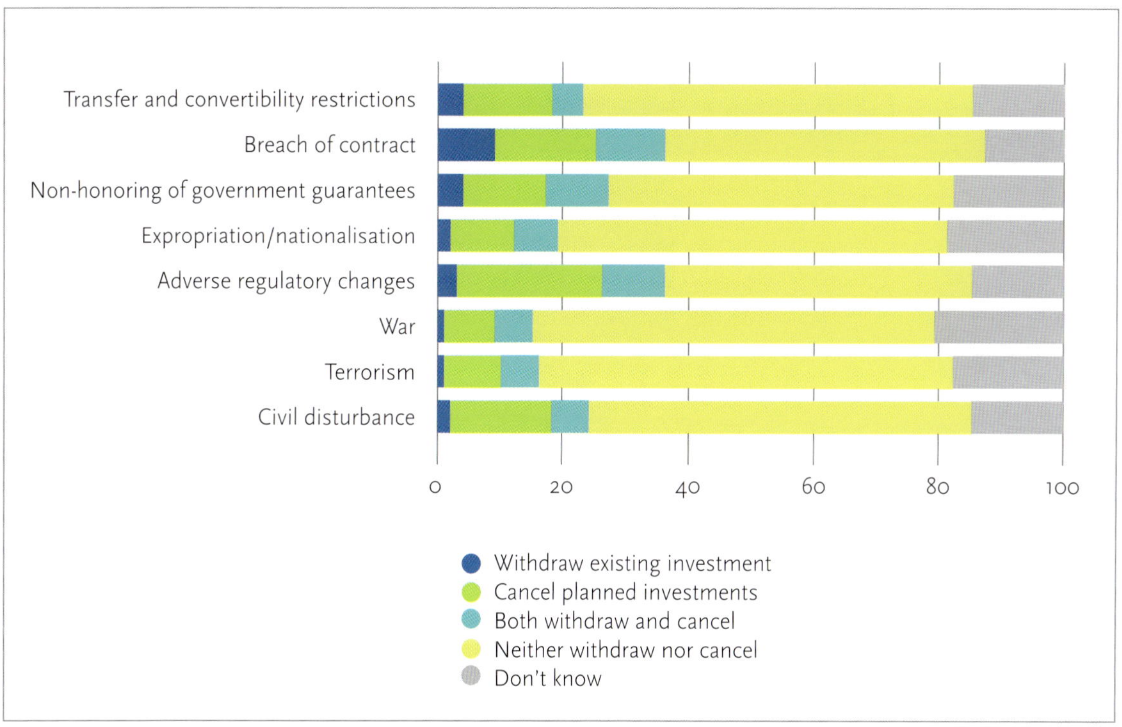

Question 8. What tools or mechanisms does your company use to mitigate political risk when investing in developing countries?

Percent of respondents

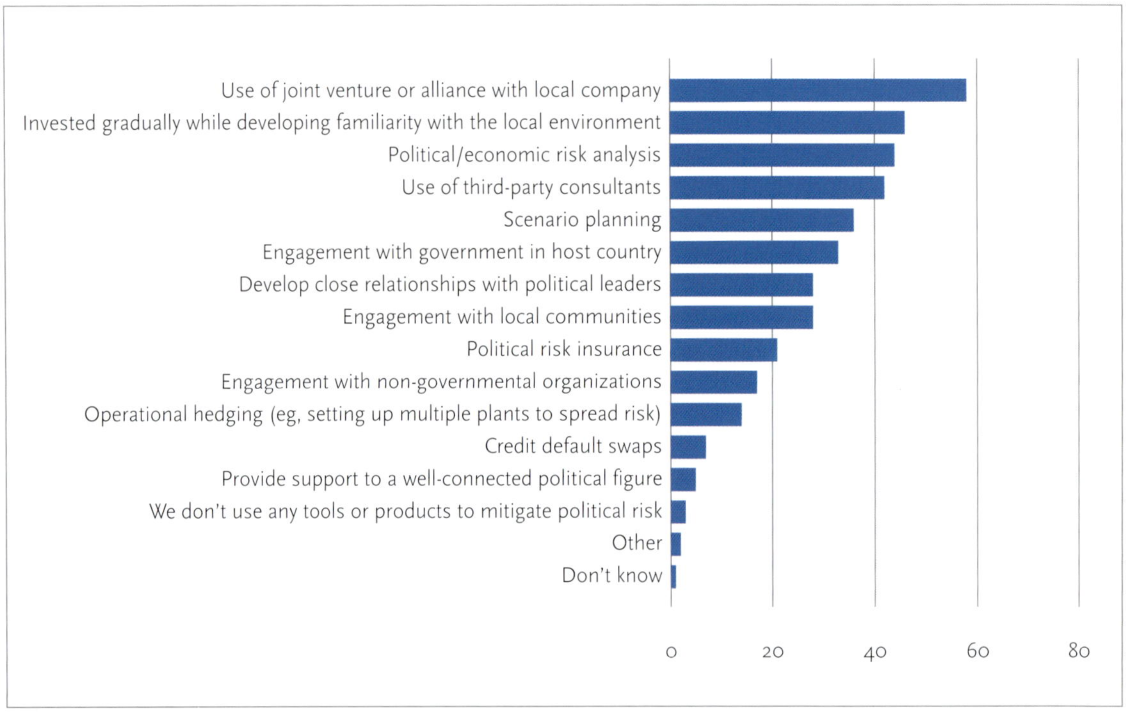

Question 9. In your opinion, in the countries where your company invests, what are the most effective tools or mechanisms available to your firm for alleviating each of the following risks?

Percent of respondents

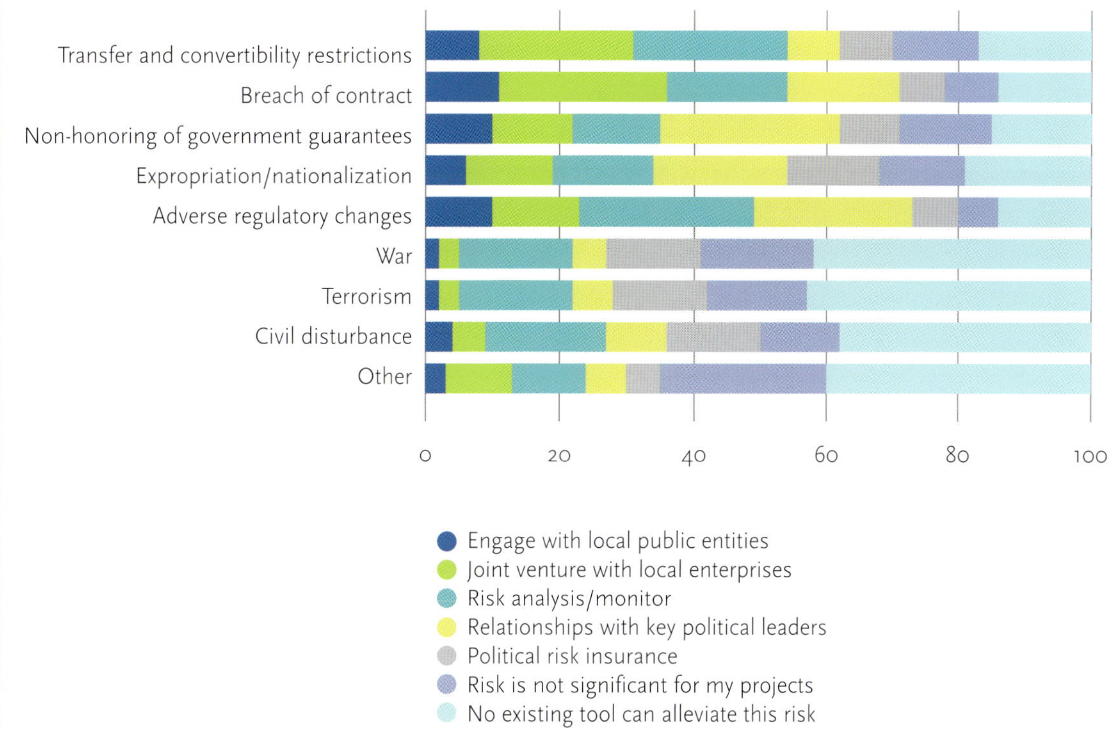

Question 10. How has the recent turmoil in the Arab World affected your plans for investments in the Middle East and North Africa (MENA) region? Select all that apply.

Percent of respondents

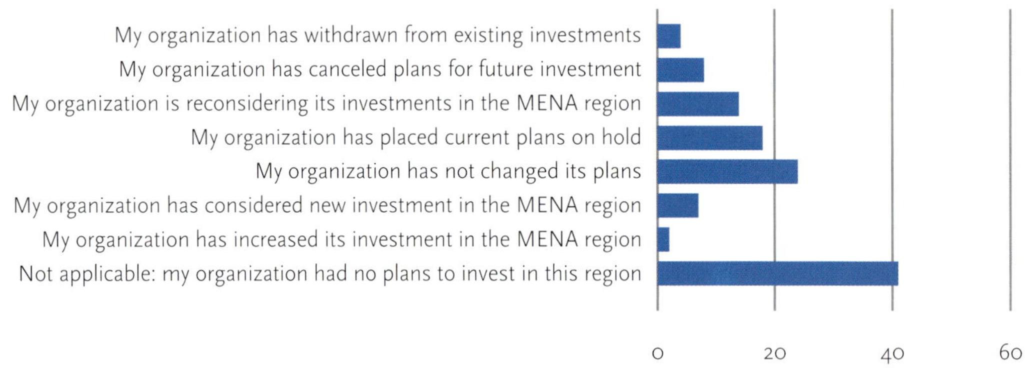

Question 11. How has the recent turmoil in the Arab World affected your perception of the following types of political risk in the MENA region?

Percent of respondent

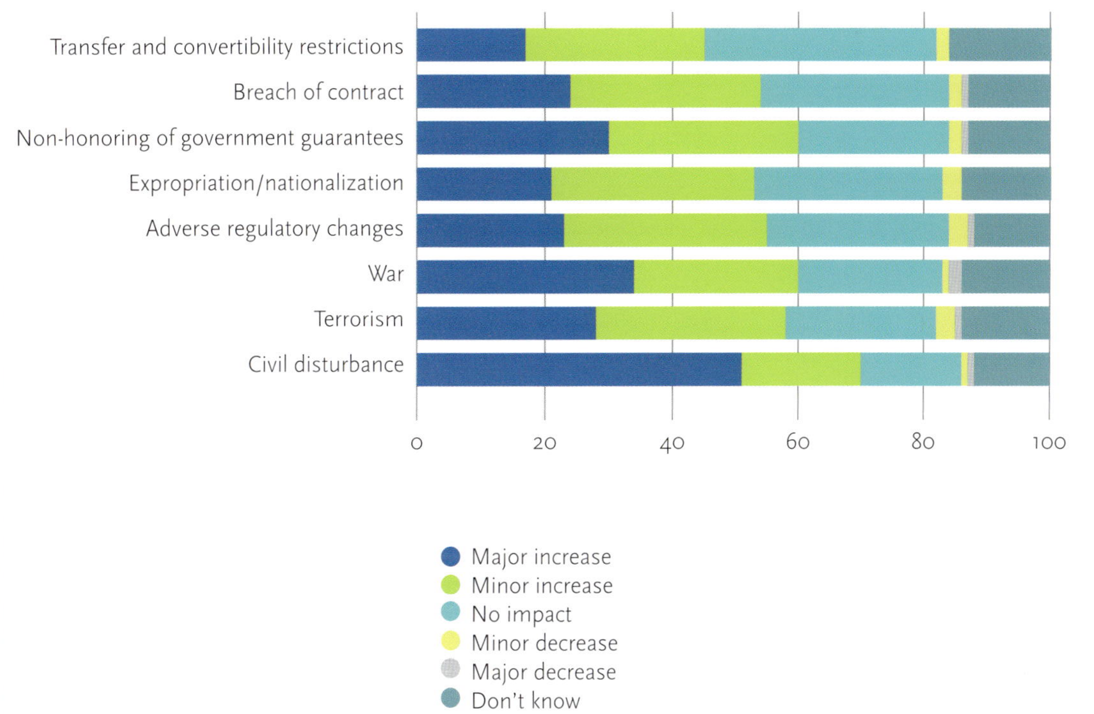

Question 12. How would the following affect your decision to invest in the MENA region? Select one for each factor.

Percent of respondents

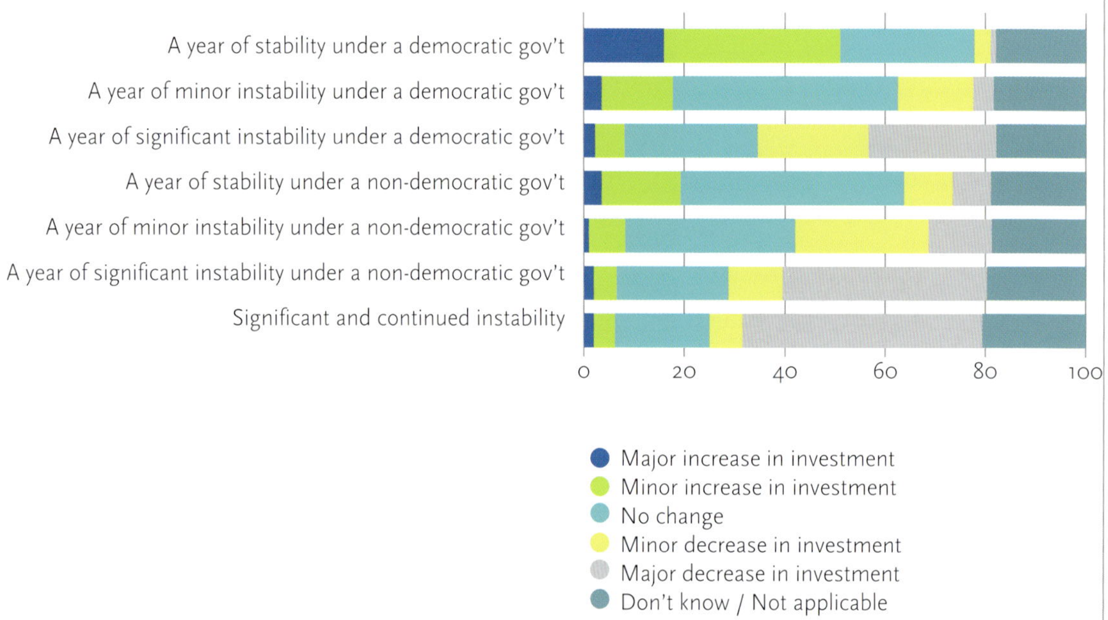

Question 13. How has the recent turmoil in the Arab World affected your plans for investments in emerging markets outside MENA?

Percent of respondents

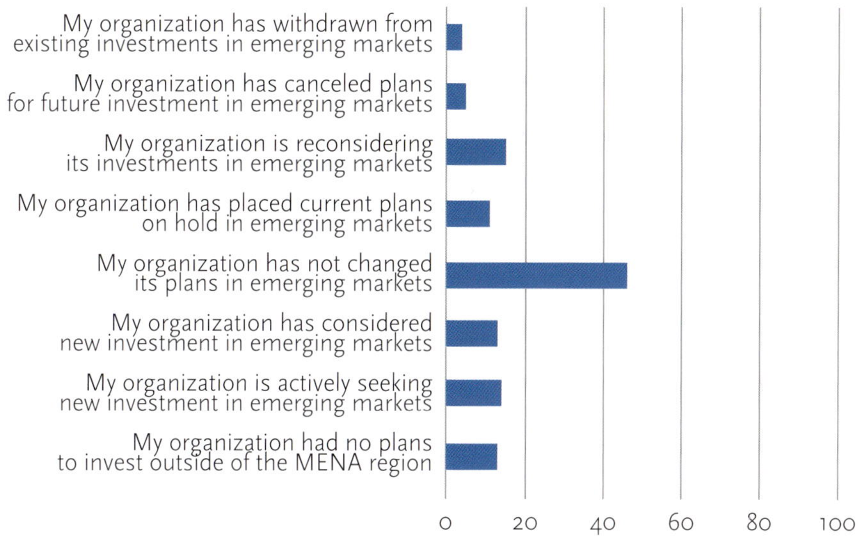

Question 14. In your opinion, which of the following is the most likely to be actively involved with an expropriation?

Percent of respondents

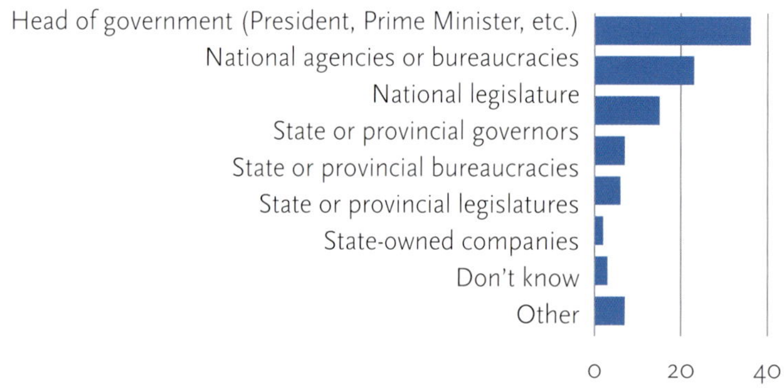

Question 15. Disputes can arise between foreign investors and government agencies. When these arise in countries where your organization is investing, how do you view the relationship between these agencies and other government entities?

Percent of respondents

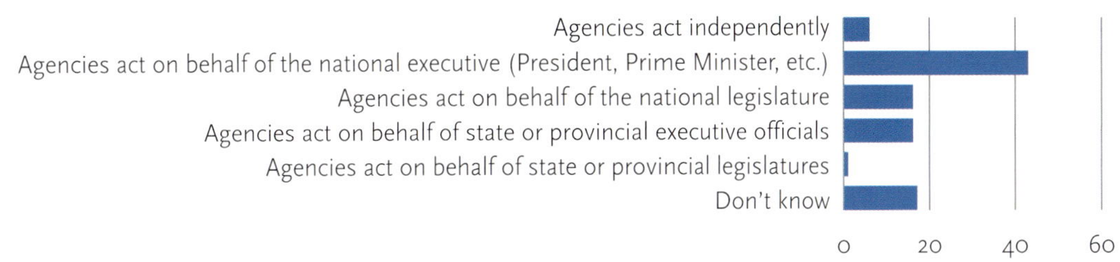

Question 16. Many countries with non-democratic governments have elected legislatures. In your opinion, how do such legislatures affect the following kinds of risk?

Percent of respondents

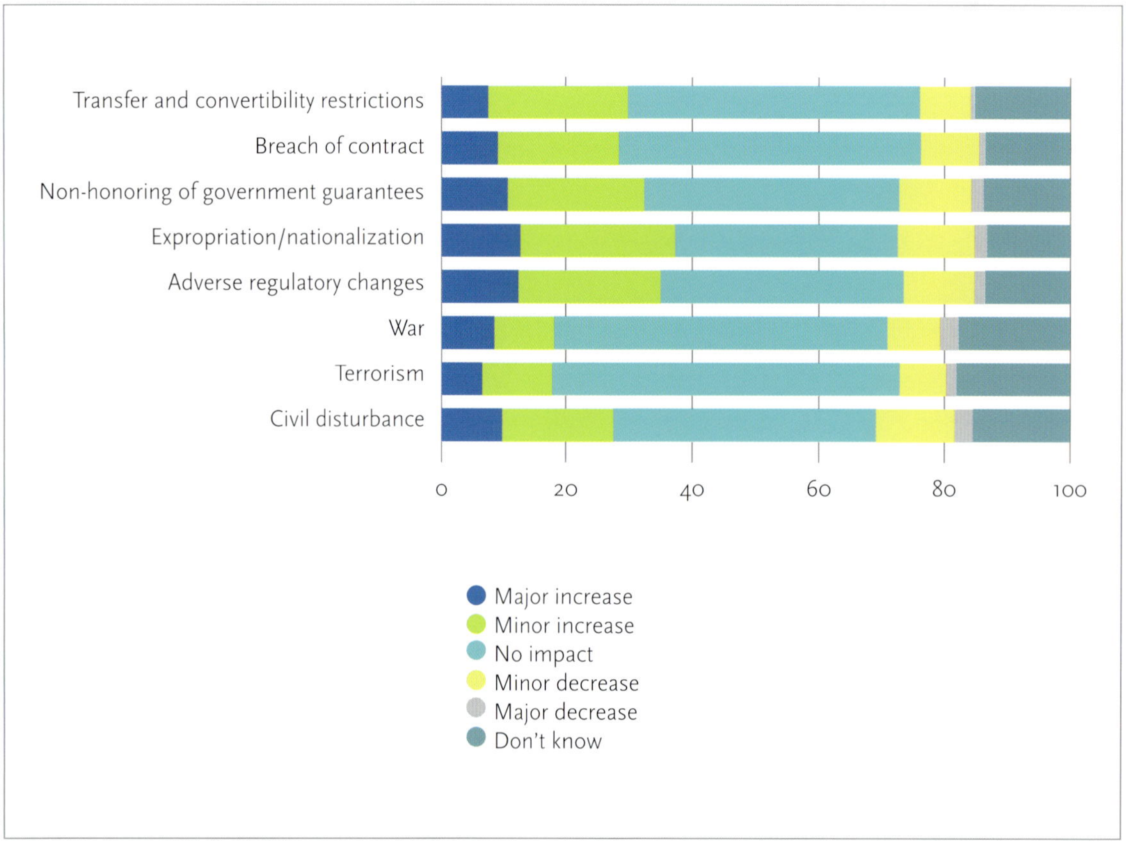

Question 17. How would the following structural market conditions affect your business's risk of expropriation?

Percent of respondents

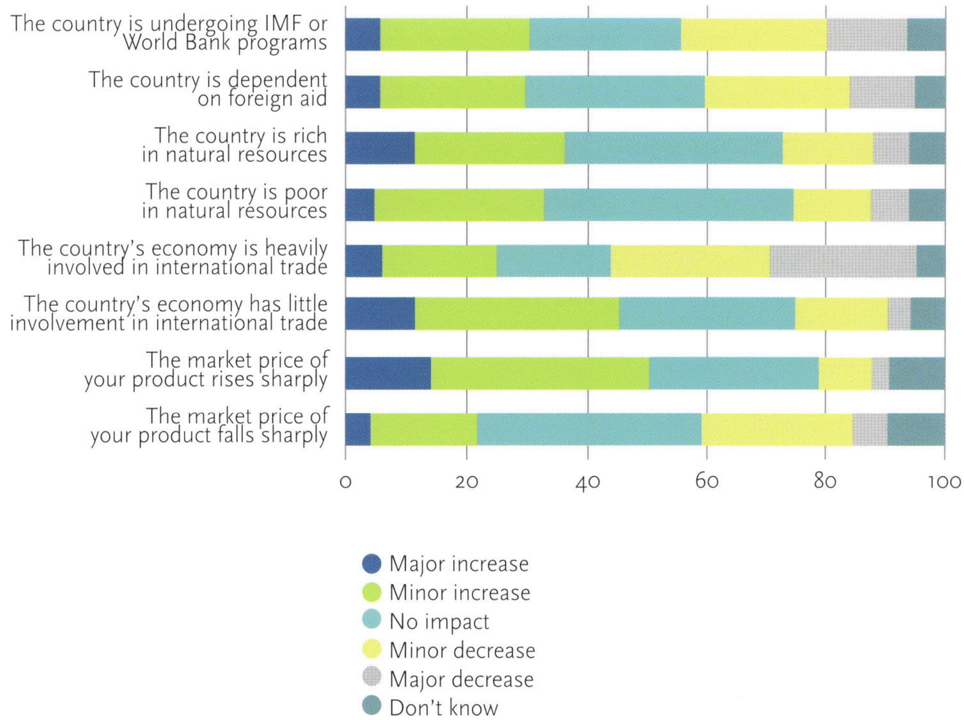

Question 18. How would the following political factors affect your business's risk of expropriation?

Percent of respondents

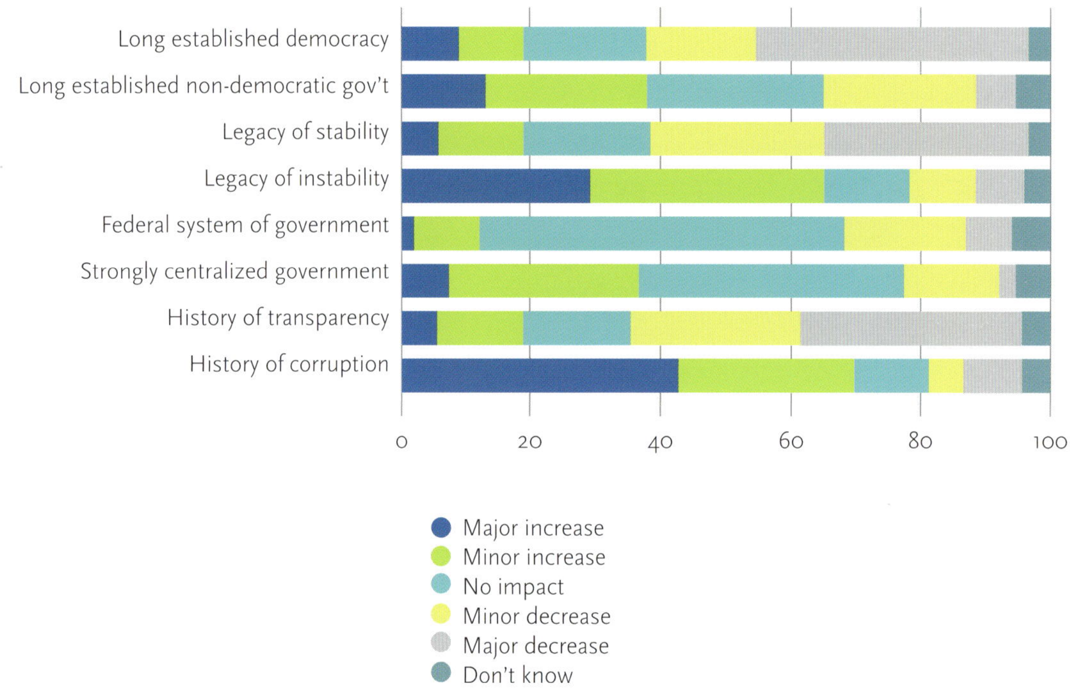

Question 19. How would the following events affect your business's risk of expropriation?

Percent of respondents

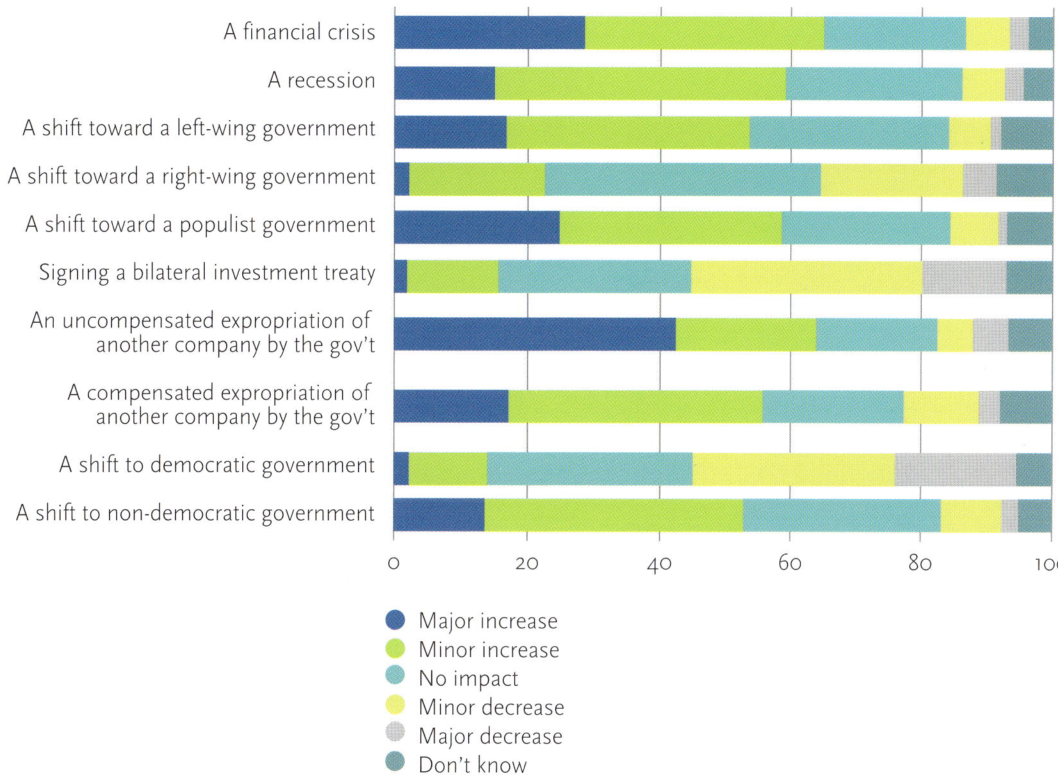

Appendix 3 Lloyd's Syndicates

Lloyd's Syndicate Members

Company	
ACE Global Markets	Kiln
Amlin	Liberty Syn. Mgmt.
Ark	O'Farrell
Ascot	Marketform
Aspen	MAP
Beazley	Novae
Catlin	Starr PFR Consortium
Chaucer	Pembroke
Hardy	QBE
Hiscox	Talbot

Appendix 4 Berne Union and Prague Club Members

Berne Union Members

Company	Country	Year joined
ASEI	Indonesia	1999
ASHRA	Israel	1958
CESCE	Spain	1972
ECGC	India	1957
ECGD	United Kingdom	1934
ECIC SA	South Africa	2004
EDC	Canada	1947
EFIC	Australia	1957
EGAP	Czech Republic	1996
EKF	Denmark	1997
EKN	Sweden	1947
EXIMBANKA SR	Slovak Republic	2004
EXIM J	Jamaica	1983
FINNVERA	Finland	1964
GIEK	Norway	1951
HKEC	Hong Kong SAR, China	1969
KSURE	Korea, Rep. of	1977
KUKE	Poland	1999
MEXIM	Malaysia	1985
MEHIB	Hungry	2000
NEXI	Japan	1970
ONDD	Belgium	1954
OPIC	United States	1974
SACE	Italy	1959
SERV	Switzerland	1956
SID	Slovenia	1998
SINOSURE	China	1996
SLECIC	Sri Lanka	1984
TEBC	Taiwan, China	1996
THAI EXIMBANK	Thailand	2003
TURK EXIMBANK	Turkey	1992
US EXIMBANK	United States	1962

Company	Country	Year joined
Private		
ATRADIUS[a]	Netherlands	1953
CGIC	South Africa	1958
CHARTIS	United States	1999
COFACE[a]	France	1948
COSEC[a]	Portugal	1977
ECICS	Singapore	1979
EH GERMANY[a]	Germany	1953
FCIA	United States	1963
HISCOX	Bermuda	2008
OEKB[a]	Austria	1955
PWC[a]	Germany	1974
SBCE[a]	Brazil	2001
SOVEREIGN	Bermuda	2001
ZURICH	United States	2001
Multilateral		
ICIEC	Multilateral	2007
MIGA	Multilateral	1992

a *Some medium- or long-term export credit insurance or investment insurance or both provided on account of the state.*

Appendix 4 Berne Union and Prague Club Members (cont'd)

Prague Club members

Company	Country	Year joined
Public		
AOFI	Serbia	2007
BAEZ	Bulgaria	1997
BECI	Botswana	2005
ECGA	Oman	2000
ECGE	Egypt, Arab Rep.	2003
ECIC SA	South Africa	2002
ECIE	United Arab Emirates	2009
EGAP	Czech Republic	1993
EGFI	Iran, Islamic Rep. of	1999
EXIM R	Romania	1993
EXIMBANKA SR	Slovak Republic	1993
EXIMGARANT	Belarus	1999
HBOR	Croatia	1997
IGA	Bosnia and Herzegovina	1999
JLGC	Jordan	2001
KECIC	Kazakhstan	2004
KREDEX	Estonia	1999
KUKE	Poland	1993
MBDP	Macedonia, FYR	1999
MEHIB	Hungary	1993
NAIFE	Sudan	2007
NZECO	New Zealand	2010
PHILEXIM	Philippines	1997
SEP	Saudi Arabia	2000
SID	Slovenia	1993
THAI EXIMBANK	Thailand	1997
UKREXIMBANK	Ukraine	2008
UZBEKINVEST	Uzbekistan	1996
VNESHECONOMBANK	Russian Federation	2008

Company	Country	Year joined
Private		
LCI	Lebanon	2009
Multilateral		
ATI	Multilateral	2002
DHAMAN	Multilateral	2000
ICIEC	Multilateral	2001